rfg|YH
The Regional Food Group for Yorkshire and Humber

Acknowledgements Jane Chamberlain; Eon Carlyle Data Services; our passionate Yorkshire chefs Brian Turner, James Martin, Richard Fox, Giorgio Alessio, Rosemary Shrager, Andrew Pern, John Topham, Richard Walton Allen, Stephanie Moon and fantastic RFGYH members - Yorkshire Dales Meat, Cropton Brewery, Ulrick and Short, Hambleton Ales, The Swaledale Cheese Company, Northern Select Foods, Cryer and Stott, E Oldroyd & Sons, Bleikers Smokehouse; all members of the RFGYH; Yorkshire Forward, the European Regional Development Fund. Images:Chris North Photography and Yorkshire Tourist Board image library; members of the Regional Food Group team. Deliciouslyorkshire Shops Local editorial by Lemon Zest PR. Design by Rubber Band.

©The Regional Food Group for Yorkshire and Humber
Published by The Regional Food Group for Yorkshire and Humber, Tadcaster, North Yorkshire

The right of The Regional Food Group for Yorkshire and Humber to be identified as the author of this work has been asserted in accordance with the Copyright, Designs and Patents Act 1988

All rights reserved. No part of this publication may be reproduced in any form or any means, without prior permission from the publisher, except by reviewers or journalists who may quote brief passages or entry details.

Printed and bound in Yorkshire on recycled stock using environmentally-friendly inks.

A CIP catalogue record for this book is available from the British Library

ISBN 978-0-9556344-0-6

deliciouslyorkshire

Contents

Foreword 4
What is Deliciouslyorkshire? 6
Deliciouslyorkshire Annual Awards Winners 9
Five Reasons to Buy Local 20
Where Can I Buy Local? 21
The Many Faces of Yorkshire 22
Traditional and Innovative 24
Food and Drink Heritage 25
Gastronomic Roadshow 26
Food for All Seasons 27
Delicious Yorkshire Recipes 28

Regions
North Yorkshire 53
    Food Highlights 54
    Members 63
South Yorkshire 101
    Food Highlights 102
    Members 107
East Yorkshire 119
    Food Highlights 120
    Members 125
West Yorkshire 139
    Food Highlights 140
    Members 147
North/North East Lincolnshire 163
    Food Highlights 164
    Members 165

Deliciouslyorkshire Breakfast Members 168
Specialist Services to the Food Industry 186
Alphabetical Index 198

Contents by Category & Region

Producers

Bakers and confectioners
North 64   South 108   East 126   West 148

Dairy and eggs
North 67   South 109   East 127   West 149

Beverages – alcoholic and non alcoholic
North 72   South 110   East 128   West 150

Fish – fresh and smoked
North 75   East 129

Fresh ingredients
North 76   East 129   West 151

Ingredient suppliers
North 78   East 129   West 152

Meat, poultry and game – fresh and smoked
North 79   South 110   East 130   West 152   N & NE Lincs 165

Pies
North 83   South 111   East 131   West 153

Prepared food
North 84   South 111   East 132   West 155   N & NE Lincs 165

Preserves, honey, condiments and spices
North 86   South 113   East 133   West 157

Hospitality

Hotel and restaurants
North 87   South 114   East 134   West 159

Outside caterers
North 91   South 115   West 159

Retailers

Deli and independent grocers
North 91   South 115   East 134   West 160

Farm shops
North 95   South 116   East 135   West 160

Distributors

North 98   South 117   East 136   N & NE Lincs 165

Deliciouslyorkshire Breakfast Members

North 168   South 179   East 180   West 180

Specialist Services to the Food Industry

187

Key to icons

- Internet Sales
- Mail Order
- Own Retail Outlets
- On Site Cafe / Restaurant
- Children's Play Area
- Site Tours / Demonstrations

Foreword

Provenance, quality, innovation and seasonality –

together these comprise the philosophy behind the **deliciouslyyorkshire**® Guide to Food and Drink.

Food is the very stuff of life and as such, eating the best you can is self care at its most basic - not to mention most pleasurable!

Top quality food, produced to high standards and with integrity by people with real passion for their work – that's what this Guide is all about.

Despite, or perhaps because of, year-round availability which has come at a cost of taste and environmental damage, increasingly we are realising the benefits of wonderfully fresh seasonal produce. Yes, it is lower in food miles, has a lower carbon footprint and is good for the local economy, but best of all it tastes good!

It has been my pleasure to meet with many of the producers in the following pages and to share in the very real pride they take in their products – recipes honed over generations, livestock lovingly tended and cared for, fruit nurtured and cosseted through the cold winters.

Our research has shown that the majority of you actively seek out food and drink from our region and would like to buy more. That's why we've developed our Deliciouslyorkshire brand which can only be used by those producing in Yorkshire and Humber. At a time when the power of regional branding is increasingly being recognised by large businesses and the multiples, it's your assurance of genuine Yorkshire produce.

I hope you find this book a useful resource. If you want to keep the 'food heroes' featured in the following pages you need to find time to source their products. While time is increasingly precious, making the effort to call into that farm shop or deli or visit that stand at the local food show will not only ensure that you and your family eat the tastiest and best local produce, but also help sustain the heritage and economy of your local community, as well as benefiting the environment.

And buying local doesn't always mean having to leave the comfort of your own home, many of our members sell direct via the internet so if your schedule doesn't allow a personal visit, visit www.deliciouslyorkshire.co.uk.

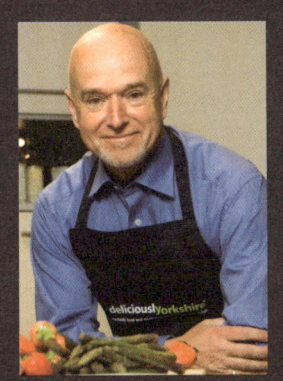

Jonathan Knight
Chief Executive
The Regional Food Group for Yorkshire and Humber

Buy Local

Buy Local, Think **deliciouslyorkshire**®

Established to indicate 'at a glance' clear regional provenance and increase awareness of the extensive range of food and drink in the region, the Deliciouslyorkshire brand can only be used by producers in Yorkshire and Humber.

The brand enables consumers interested in issues such as local sourcing, freshness, traceability and seasonal produce to actively seek out Yorkshire and Humber produce.

Research shows that awareness of the Deliciouslyorkshire brand has increased within the region by 81% (to 18%) and nationally by an impressive 31% (to 8%) according to new research*.

Yorkshire products taste better, are linked to the community and offer value for money. 96% of people that frequent independent retailers felt that food sourced from Yorkshire was more sustainable, and they felt better buying that produce.

And with the increasing demand for local produce and the quality of food and drink on offer in Yorkshire, Deliciouslyorkshire looks firmly on track for further growth.

*The research was carried out throughout January 2007 and commissioned by the Regional Food Group for Yorkshire & Humber

008
deliciouslyyorkshire

deliciouslyorkshire Awards

deliciouslyorkshire annual awards Winner 2006

Yorkshire and Humber's Finest Recognised by Deliciouslyorkshire Awards

deliciouslyorkshire Awards

The region's produce continues to be among the most innovative and delicious in the country and the annual Deliciouslyorkshire Awards are a public celebration of the very best of Yorkshire and Humber's food and drink.

Established two years ago, our awards celebrate the passionate, driven people behind that exceptional produce – enabling our members to step back from the hard work, bask in the recognition of what they have achieved and enjoy a well-deserved pat on the back.

An independent panel of expert judges carried out blind tastings and selected the nine eventual well-deserved winners from a huge range of entries from across the region. The consumption of and interest in regional foods has really flourished in the past few years and all award winners can use the distinctive and increasingly highly regarded Deliciouslyorkshire brand on packaging and promotional material.

For a special occasion or just for something a little different, why not try one of the following products from our list of Deliciouslyorkshire Winners in 2006?

And for the very latest on our next eagerly anticipated annual awards, visit our website www.deliciouslyorkshire.co.uk.

deliciously yorkshire annual awards Winner 2006

deliciously yorkshire Awards

Yorkshire Product of the Year

Winner:
E Oldroyd & Sons for Yorkshire Rhubarb

A family business with more than five generations experience in growing high quality fruit and vegetables, including traditionally grown Yorkshire indoor rhubarb. Popular seasonal tours and talks are available where rhubarb can be seen growing in the dark and harvested by candlelight.

What the judges said:

"This product has the strongest Yorkshire identity – it has heritage, tradition, history and superb simplicity."

Contact:
Janet Oldroyd Hulme
E Oldroyd & Sons, Hopefield Farm, The Shutts,
Leadwell Lane, Rothwell, West Yorkshire LS26 0ST
T: 0113 282 2245
E: eoldroyd@btconnect.com

Available through good retail outlets, as well as by mail order in season.
For full details see pages 49 and 151.

deliciously yorkshire Awards

deliciously yorkshire annual awards Winner 2006

Best Use of Regional Produce in a Menu

Winner:

The Pipe and Glass Inn, near Beverley

Chef and proprietor James Mackenzie has built up a truly enviable reputation at this recently renovated and specially situated gastro pub. Choose from the likes of locally sourced rib of Skerne beef with Yorkshire pudding and ginger burnt cream with stewed Yorkshire rhubarb.

What the judges said:

"They have got flair & passion, and despite the fact that it's harder for them to source local produce they are cutting edge in their innovative use of local produce."

For full details see pages 121 and 134.

Contact:

James Mackenzie
The Pipe & Glass Inn, West End, South Dalton,
Beverley, East Yorkshire HU17 7PN
T: 01430 810 246
E: email@pipeandglass.co.uk
W: www.pipeandglass.co.uk

deliciousyorkshire annual awards Winner 2006

deliciousyorkshire Awards

Deliciouslyorkshire Breakfast Scheme Member

Winner:

Low Penhowe, Burythorpe, near Malton

A traditional Yorkshire stone-built farmhouse with stunning views overlooking the Howardian Hills, Castle Howard and the North Yorkshire Moors, Low Penhowe makes an idyllic spot for a quiet few nights away.

What the judges said:

"Proud of their provenance and passionate about their business and Yorkshire produce, their breakfast looks appetising and well presented."

For full details see page 173.

Contact:
Christopher Turner
Low Penhowe, Burythorpe, Malton,
North Yorkshire YO17 9LU
T: 01653 658 336
E: lowpenhowebandb@aol.com
W: www.bedandbreakfastyorkshire.co.uk

deliciouslyorkshire

013

deliciouslyYorkshire Awards

Large Producer of the Year

Winner:
Mackenzies Yorkshire Smokehouse, Blubberhouses, Yorkshire

Set amidst the beautiful Blubberhouses Moor, lies Mackenzies Yorkshire Smokehouse, a family business creating superb smoked fish, poultry, meats and a complete fine Deli foods selection using traditional methods of curing and smoking. All products are free from artificial colours and flavours.

What the judges said:
"Strong regionality, excellent use of branding, solid business growth over the past few years and a positive business and marketing plan."

Available through farmers markets, independent delis and own retail outlet as well as by mail and internet order.
For full details see page 81.

deliciouslyYorkshire annual awards Winner 2006

Contact:
Robert Crowson, Mackenzies Yorkshire Smokehouse, Units 1-6 Hardisty Hill, Blubberhouses, North Yorkshire LS21 2PQ
T: 01943 880 369
E: yorkshire.smokehouse@virgin.net
W: www.mackenziesyorkshiresmokehouse.co.uk

deliciouslyyorkshire annual awards *Winner 2006*

deliciouslyyorkshire Awards

Small Food Producer of the Year

Winner:

Stamfrey Farm Organics, West Rounton, Northallerton

Deliciously thick and award-winning creamy organic clotted cream and drinking/pouring yogurt, handmade using traditional methods on their dairy farm.

What the judges said:

"This company's passion, innovative and entrepreneurial skills make them stand out ahead of the crowd."

Contact:

Sue Gaudie
Stamfrey Farm Organics, Stamfrey Farm,
West Rounton, Northallerton, North Yorkshire DL6 2LJ
T: 01609 882 297
E: sue@gaudie.com
W: www.stamfrey.com

Available through independent delis, food shows and farmers markets.
For full details see page 69.

deliciouslyyorkshire

deliciouslyYorkshire Awards

deliciouslyYorkshire annual awards Winner 2006

Best Marketing Campaign

Winner:
Debbie & Andrew's Sausages, Thirsk, North Yorkshire

Sausages are close to Debbie and Andrew's hearts. They have a passion for fresh ingredients, good, lean pork and delicate herbs, spices and seasoning – and nothing but the best goes into every sausage produced.

What the judges said:

"Thought very hard about their customer. Stuck to their roots, they have a strong belief in the product. Gave away products to schools following the Jamie Oliver TV programmes, to challenge the assumption that their products are unhealthy. They clearly know where they are going."

Available through independent delis, supermarkets, by mail order and internet sales. **For full details see pages 61 and 79.**

Contact:
Andrew Keeble
Debbie and Andrews Ltd,
Thirsk, North Yorkshire YO7 3TD
T: 0800 783 6481
E: andrew@debbieandandrews.co.uk
W: www.debbieandandrews.co.uk

deliciously yorkshire annual awards Winner 2006

deliciously yorkshire Awards

Independent Retailer of the Year

Winner:

Lewis & Cooper, Northallerton

An award-winning and internationally renowned gourmet emporium which remains a family business. Thousands of rare treats including their Gold Great Taste Award winner and definite number one foodie treat handmade plum pudding, packed with succulent fruits and generously laced with Hennessey Cognac and manufactured by hand to a secret century-old recipe.

What the judges said:

"A well established business, constantly evolving with a unique atmosphere. Local sourcing is a high commitment. Strong point of sale merchandising. Embodies local Yorkshire food retailing – a bit special."

Available through the Northallerton store, food shows, independent delis, as well as by mail and internet order.
For full details see page 92.

Contact:
Victoria Kaye
Lewis & Cooper, 92 High Street,
Northallerton, North Yorkshire DL7 8PP
T: 01609 772 880
E: sales@lewisandcooper.co.uk
W: www.lewisandcooper.co.uk

deliciously yorkshire

deliciously yorkshire Awards

deliciously yorkshire annual awards Winner 2006

Farm Shop of the Year

Winner:
The Farmer's Cart, York

The freshest vegetables, soft fruits and salad crops harvested daily from the surrounding fields, which provide idyllic surroundings to the shop and tearoom. Light lunches, cream teas, freshly baked cakes and other delicious treats produced from its own seasonal produce. School tours, birthday parties and seasonal events including an Easter egg hunt, sheep shearing demonstrations and famous 'Pumpkin Fest and Haunted Hayrides'.

What the judges said:
"Consistent commitment to and excellent merchandising of regional produce."

For full details see page 96.

Contact:
Margaret Sykes
The Farmer's Cart, Towthorpe Grange,
Towthorpe Lane, York YO32 9ST
T: 01904 499 183
E: thefarmerscart@btconnect.com
W: www.thefarmerscart.co.uk

deliciouslyyorkshire annual awards Winner 2006

deliciouslyyorkshire Awards

Most Innovative Product

Winner:

Voakes Pies for Pork Pie
with Black Pudding & Red Onion Marmalade

Award-winning pork pies made using pork from the Voakes' own herd of pigs and only the best quality ingredients. A delicious pork pie for food lovers who appreciate a traditional premium pie.

What the judges said:

"Stunning, innovative could put on a Yorkshire Ploughman's plate, not flash, nice with a pint of real ale on a Saturday before the match."

Contact:
Andrew Voakes
Voakes Pies, Whixley Grange, Whixley, York YO26 8AY
T: 01423 339 988
E: enquiries@voakespies.co.uk
W: www.voakespies.com

Available through good retailers and direct to the public at food shows and farmers markets. More information on the website.
For full details see page 84.

Buy Local

Five reasons to Buy Local

Buying local contributes on many levels – socially, economically, environmentally and to our health.

- **Provenance** – know exactly where your food comes from, the sustainable methods used to produce it and meet the people who produce it

- **Low food miles** – the shorter the distance from field to fork, the fewer the food miles. Around 40% of the lorries on our roads are transporting food, contributing to congestion and pollution

- **Value for money** – direct sales, or those through local outlets, reduce producers overheads enabling savings to be passed on to customers

- **Protect the environment** – by encouraging sustainable methods of production and reduced packaging

- **Support the local economy** – buying food produced locally, whether from the producer or from a local outlet boosts the local economy

deliciouslyyorkshire

Buy Local

Where can I Buy Local?

- **Local High Street** – use it or lose it. Look out for butchers who specialise in local meat. They will be able to tell you which farm your Sunday joint comes from and offer advice on how to get the very best flavour out of it. Ask your greengrocer for local seasonal fruit and vegetables: buy fresh carrots 'with the muck still on' and taste the difference

- **Farm Shops** – perfect for those who like to know exactly where their food comes from. Raised and nurtured by their own hands – often with advice on how to get the best out of them and even a recipe!

- **Farmers Markets** – a revival of the traditional markets of old. Enjoy the hustle and bustle of market trading, while buying something that couldn't be fresher

- **Local Shows** – see a wide range of local produce and meet the producers at shows throughout the region (see Calendar of Foodie Events on page 195) or visit www.deliciouslyyorkshire.co.uk

- **Supermarkets** – who continue to work towards developing the ranges of the local food offering

- **Online** – many producers now sell via the internet so either take a look at their individual websites or visit www.deliciouslyyorkshire.co.uk to find your nearest retailer

Faces of Yorkshire

The Many Faces of Yorkshire

Wild, expansive, tranquil, charming and awesome, Yorkshire – 'God's Own County' – and Humber – its eastern coastline – is many different things to different people.

One of England's largest counties, Yorkshire is also one of its most beautiful, offering many faces and just as many moods. From the North York Moors National Park and the Dales complete with intricate network of dry stone walling, to the glories of one of the finest stretches of coastline in Britain – all with a rich heritage to match!

Ancient castles and stately homes stand proud over rolling acres of countryside, atmospheric ruined abbeys and bleak historic sites of epic civil war battles speak of struggles for the hearts and minds of the region's people. The monumentally impressive minster's of York, Beverley and Ripon continue to inspire the same sense of awe and wonder as they ever did.

From the bleak and lonely moorland of the Brontes to the pretty pastoral leafy lanes of Heriot country; towering cliffs, smugglers' coves, bustling fishing ports and golden beaches to picturesque dales villages that seem to spring from the landscape; cobbled market towns to chic and sophisticated city waterfronts – from the traditional to the innovative, Yorkshire has it all and more.

deliciouslyorkshire

023

deliciouslyyorkshire

Traditional and Innovative

Although it has justly claimed its place in history, the region is just as forward-thinking and relevant today as it ever was. Market towns such as Ripon and Beverley are thriving in providing something different from the average high street, while the floral town of Harrogate with its rich spa heritage and the city of Leeds offer everything that could be needed by the most keen of fashionistas. York is ideal for boutique shopping amidst medieval architecture and hosts Britain's largest annual Festival of Food and Drink each September.

Farmers markets are a phenomenal success throughout the region and many towns and cities have vibrant weekly markets showcasing the best of local produce, although not all of them can claim Sheffield's pedigree – the city has been hosting markets for more than seven hundred years.

Food and Drink Heritage

And it has a rich food and drink heritage to match.

If you want to eat out, you're in luck. Whether you're looking for traditional tearooms or vibrant pavement cafés, cutting-edge gastro pubs or Michelin-starred restaurants, all the major cities have a lively food and drink scene.

It is no accident that Yorkshire is the nation's largest producer of food. It is a landscape that has been inextricably shaped by farming and food production over successive generations.

From the rhubarb forcing sheds that sprang up almost as a by-product of the textile industry during the industrial revolution – the fertile natural 'manure' produced by Yorkshire sheep and 'shoddy' wool waste from the Leeds and Bradford woollen industry, being a perfect nitrogen-rich growing medium – to the fertile green pastures of the Yorkshire Dales that gave rise to delicious farmhouse cheeses such as that Wallace and Gromit favourite, Wensleydale.

From outside the region, it would be easy to believe that Yorkshire and Humber food is all about such substantial and traditional fayre such as the eponymous crispy, golden Yorkshire pudding (apparently devised to make the meat go further, but no less tasty for that), creamy sweet curd tarts and the succulent York Ham for which the county is renowned.

And they are delicious, of course. But there's much more to Yorkshire produce and, contrary to the national archetype of the parsimonious Yorkshire man or woman (which, in these parts, we prefer to call sensible 'thriftiness'), with typical Yorkshire hospitality, we want to share some of our finest culinary ideas with you!

Yorkshire and Humber has always occupied a prominent place in the nation's food awareness with produce that is not only bountiful but also of an unsurpassed quality. Despite our nation's over-reliance on imported foods of all descriptions, mouth-watering ingredients continue to be produced in the farms and fields of Yorkshire and Humber. And as any chef knows, the very best dishes can only be made using the very best ingredients.

deliciously yorkshire

Gastronomic Roadshow

Our gastronomic roadshow starts in North Yorkshire, famous for its robust cheeses, niche micro breweries and award-winning ice cream; through to East Yorkshire with its delicious fudges, delicate goats cheeses and tangy dressings; West Yorkshire's inimitable curries, English hedgerow wines and award-winning meat-packed pies and South Yorkshire with its burgeoning local market scene and the fabulous fresh fish from the fishing ports of North and North East Lincolnshire.

Sizzling sausages, North Sea turbot, Whitby crab, smoked salmon and meats, an array of meat from award-winning Limestone Beef and omega-packed venison to rare breed pork and lamb, crunchy vegetables, cider made by monks and in reclaimed orchards. The list is endless.

Yorkshire people have always had a fondness for sweet confections too and its baked goods are unsurpassed, from crusty loaves to sticky cakes. Yorkshire is justly famous for liquorice – the sticky black stuff has been made in the town of Pontefract since medieval times – but also boasts makers of handmade chocolates, fudges, toffees, preserves and bottled fruits of all kinds. It is a county where entrepreneurs take the best of the traditional and improve upon it.

Food for All Seasons

Yorkshire country life has always been marked by the seasons – who can resist the first of the zingy spears of forced pink rhubarb which brighten up the coldest days of winter or the first asparagus of the short season in early May? Now it seems the rest of the world is catching up! Seasonality, provenance, low carbon footprint, the survival of local communities – are all key issues. The answer is clear – and points to buying more locally. And what a choice!

Our ambition is simple – to help you maximise the pleasure you derive from food. We aim to help those who increasingly care about local provenance, low food miles and environmental impact – in other words are seeking fresh tasty, real food – to make more informed choices more easily.

Whether you choose to build a direct relationship with a supplier or support small scale producers through farmers markets, local shows, farm shops and independent retailers and delis, often the most terrific producers and shops are right under your nose.

And how much more local can you get than shopping for some of these fantastic foods on your doorstep or in your own home online?

www.deliciouslyyorkshire.co.uk

deliciouslyyorkshire

Recipes

Butter Roasted Breast of Yorkshire Quail on a Waldorf Salad with a Green Apple Dressing............................. 29

Red Pepper Chutney Tart.. 30

Slow-Cooked Yorkshire Belly Pork 32

East Coast Velvet Wolfish Linguine al 'Arneis e Tartufo' 34

Silky Swaledale Goats Cheese Soufflé 36

Fillet of North Sea Halibut with Buttered Sand Hutton Asparagus, 'Bleikers' Smoked Salmon and Tartare Veloute 37

Rosemary-Raisin Sponge Cake, with Honeyed Lowna Dairy Goats Cheese 38

Apricot and Raisin Cheesecake... 39

Yorkshire Tapas... 40

Braised Yorkshire Dales Shin Beef 42

Sirloin Steak Stuffed with Cropton Beer Marinated Cheese 43

½ Fat Blueberry Muffins with Delyte 5 44

Casserole of Beef in 'Nightmare'.. 45

Swaledale Goat's Cheese and Pancetta en Croute with Apple Chutney 46

Creme Bruleé with a Nutty Ice 47

Yorkshire Ruby Gold Cheese Smoked Chicken and Avocado Salad.. 48

Chicken Tikka in Rhubarb Mayonnaise... 49

Romanov Salmon 50

Butter Roasted Breast of Yorkshire Quail on a Waldorf Salad with a Green Apple Dressing

Brian Turner

Brian Turner is one of Britain's most successful and well-known chefs. In addition to running highly respected restaurants in the UK, he is a successful television personality, appearing regularly on 'Ready Steady Cook' and 'Great Food Live'.

Recipe information
Serves: 4
Cooking time: 8-10 minutes

Ingredients
4 large crowns of Yorkshire quail
2oz butter
2oz mirepoix (diced carrot & onion)
1 tsp chopped basil
1 tbsp walnut oil
8oz celery
1 green apple
1 tbsp mayonnaise
½ tbsp crème fraiche
4-6 whole walnuts
4 sprigs chervil
Salt & pepper
2 tbsp light olive oil
½ lemon
2 splashes green Tabasco sauce

Method
French trim the winglets of the quail and remove the wishbone.

Chop the basil leaves and mix with the walnut oil.

Sear the skins of the quail. Brush with the basil and walnut mix. Brush regularly.

Chop the onions and carrot for mirepoix. Place in the roasting dish. Stand the quail crown on top, season and roast in hot oven 200°C for 8-10 minutes, keep pink. Take out of oven and out of dish and keep warm.

Meanwhile clean the green apple, cut a thin $1/8$" slice and cut into a dice. Put into lemon juice.

Cut the rest of the apple into small batons and place into mayonnaise, add crème fraiche. Peel and cut celery into same size batons and add to mix. Add broken up walnuts. Mix and check seasoning. Spoon into middle of bowl.

Mix green dice of apple and lemon juice with olive oil and season with Tabasco.

Take off breasts of bird and lay on salad.

Spoon dressing over, lay sprig of chervil on top and serve.

Red Pepper Chutney Tart

James Martin

Celebrity chef James Martin was brought up in Yorkshire and is the host of BBC1's 'Saturday Kitchen'. He is author of a number of books, most recently 'The Great British Village Show Cookbook' and 'Sweet Baby James'.

deliciously**yorkshire**

Red Pepper Chutney Tart

Peppers are so versatile and full of flavour as well as being an excellent source of vitamin C. They come in a variety of colours red, green, yellow and orange, all of which have a different flavour. The green ones are strong with a distinct edge to their flavour, making them slightly bitter, the orange and yellow peppers are often lightly flavoured by comparison. But it's the red ones that I have used for this dish because they have a sweet more rounded flavour. One of the best things about peppers is that they taste great raw so mixing them in a salad or salsa adds extra flavour. They also feature in a wide variety of cooked dishes such as gazpacho, ratatouille and piperada. When you buy peppers or grow them only pick the firm glossy ones and avoid the ones that are wrinkly and soft. When you prepare peppers cut them in half and remove the stalk and seeds and also the white fibrous rib as this can be quite sour and turns bitter when cooked.

Recipe information

Serves: 4
Prep time: 25 minutes
Cooking time: 28 minutes approx

Ingredients

200g ready rolled puff pastry
2 large red peppers, seeded and cut into strips
140ml olive oil
2 tsp liquid honey
25g grain mustard
3 tbsp white wine vinegar
1 onion, peeled and finely diced
3 garlic cloves, peeled and diced
200ml brown chicken stock
50g shaved parmesan cheese

Method

Preheat the oven to 180°C/350°F/Gas Mark 4.

Sear the peppers in 4 tbsp of the olive oil for 3 minutes. Add the honey, vinegar, sliced onion and garlic, cover and then allow to simmer over a medium heat for 10 minutes until the peppers soften. Remove from the heat and add the remaining olive oil and the stock. Season to taste and set aside.

Cut the puff pastry into 3" circles, place onto a baking tray and prick each circle 3-4 times with a fork then cover with greaseproof paper and on top of that place another tray. This is so the pastry can cook but without rising too much. Then bake in the oven for 10-12 minutes or until evenly golden brown, remove and allow to cool.

When cool brush each base with the grain mustard then spoon the pepper chutney on top. With a potato peeler peel the parmesan cheese and lay on top. Place the tarts back into the oven for 2-3 minutes to melt the cheese then remove and serve.

Slow-Cooked Yorkshire Belly Pork

Richard Fox

Richard Fox is a food and beer writer and broadcaster, appears regularly on both radio and TV and is winner of the British Guild of Beer Writers Award for food and beer writing. He is author of 'The Food and Beer Cook Book'.

Slow-Cooked Yorkshire Belly Pork

The only way to cook belly pork is long and slow. Not only does this make it melt-in-the-mouth tender, but also lends itself perfectly to the addition of a full-flavoured, robustly strong English ale, where the beer flavours have got time to really penetrate and flavour the meat.

A gloriously rustic dish, best served with a huge bowl of mash. Pile the slices of pork on a big chopping board along with the ribs, and pour all the sauce and veg into a soup tureen with ladle.

Recipe information
Serves: 4
Prep time: 20 minutes
Cooking time: 4 hours

Ingredients
1 kg belly pork, preferably with the bone still intact
2 carrots
1 stick celery
½ onion
3 cloves garlic
Fennel stalks (from 2 bulbs)
1 leek
300ml water
330ml Yorkshire beer
½ chicken stock cube
1 bay leaf
3 sprigs rosemary
1 tin chopped tomatoes

For the dry marinade:
1 dsp chopped oregano
1 dsp chopped parsley
1 dsp chopped rosemary
1 clove garlic, finely chopped
1 heaped tsp sea salt
Freshly ground black pepper

Method

Pre-heat the oven to 160°C. Score the skin of the belly pork with a series of criss-cross diagonal slashes. You will need an extremely sharp knife, or an artist's scalpel. Combine all the dry marinade ingredients and rub into the slashed surface of the skin – as if you're giving a massage!

Chop all the remaining vegetables and put in the bottom of a roasting tin, big enough to accommodate the belly pork. Place the belly pork on the veg and pour in the beer and the tinned tomatoes. Add the water until it comes about ⅔ of the way up the side of the meat. Add the herbs and put in the oven for about 4 hours. Remove from the oven and set aside to rest for no less than fifteen minutes – this allows the meat to relax and the meat juices to flow into the sauce giving added flavour.

After resting, remove the belly and place on a chopping board. With a sharp knife, carefully cut the whole slab of meat away from the ribs. Then pull and cut away the crackling and set aside for garnish. If the crackling is not crispy enough, just turn the oven up to 200°C and put it back in the oven for about ten minutes (after separating it from the meat). Carve the meat into approximately 1½ cm slices – you'll need a really sharp knife, but don't worry if the meat falls apart a little – this is all about flavour, not fancy presentation. Serve up the ribs as well – there's stacks of juicy, succulent meat between each one just gagging to be knawed off the bone!

East Coast Velvet Wolfish Linguine al 'Arneis e Tartufo'

Giorgio Alessio

La Lanterna

Italian-born Giorgio Alessio has run award-winning Scarborough restaurant La Lanterna for ten years and is author of 'White Truffle Yorkshire Pudding'.

East Coast Velvet Wolfish Linguine al 'Arneis e Tartufo'

Recipe information

Serves:
4 generously or 6 as a starter

Prep time: 35 minutes

Cooking time: 2-3¼ hours
(to simmer the stock)

Ingredients

For the velvet crab stock:
6 East Coast velvet crabs
1 onion
1 celery
1 carrot
2 bay leaves
Salt & pepper

For the tajarin:
(extra fine hand-made egg pasta from Piemonte)
00 flour
3 free range eggs
Scarborough wolfish fillets
(or any other firm white fish)
Extra virgin olive oil
Finely chopped garlic
Fresh basil
Cherry tomatoes - cut into quarters
1 glass arneis (white wine from the Langhe region)
Knob of butter
Salt & pepper
1 medium size black truffle
Fresh thyme - to garnish

Method

Add all the ingredients for the stock into a large pan with 2 litres of water. Simmer for 2-3 hours.

Make the dough for the tajarin and allow to rest for approx. ½ hour.

Put a drop of the olive oil in to a frying pan on a low heat, coat the fish with the plain flour and fry the fish on both sides until they start to brown. Add a teaspoon of finely chopped garlic, add the cherry tomatoes and sauté for a few seconds, add the wine and a little stock. Allow to reduce slightly, add the butter, sprinkle with fresh basil, then place in an oven-proof dish and keep warm.

Make the tajarin – you will need a manual pasta machine.

Using the remaining crab stock, bring to the boil and add the fresh pasta to the stock. Cook for 10-12 seconds.

Drain the pasta and lay it on top of the fish in the oven-proof dish.

Grill for a few minutes until it has a light crust.

Shave with slivers of fresh black truffle !!

Garnish the dish with the fresh thyme.

Silky Swaledale Goats Cheese Soufflé

Rosemary Shrager

Rosemary's professional career includes a period working for Pierre Koffman at the internationally famous Tante Claire restaurant in London and also a period working for Jean-Christophe Novelli and was Head Chef at Amhuinnsuidhe Castle until 2002. Passionate about food she now runs her renowned cookery course at her cookery school based at Swinton Park, Masham. Her cookery book, 'Rosemary - Castle Cook' has been described as "an object lesson in handling the finest produce".

Recipe information
Serves: 4
Cooking time: 20 minutes

Ingredients
150g Swaledale goats cheese
2 egg yolks
5 egg whites
Freshly ground black pepper
Handful of walnuts, finely chopped
200ml double cream
4 sprigs chervil
Handful of rocket leaves

For the béchamel:
20g butter
20g plain flour
100ml milk
Pinch cayenne

Method
Oven 190°C.

First make the béchamel, melt the butter in a small pan over a low heat, add the flour and cook for 30 seconds. Add the milk and continue stirring until thick, now add 100g of the goats cheese, mix well until the cheese has completely melted. Set aside.

Butter 4 ramekins, coat with soft butter, now sprinkle with walnuts and put into the fridge until required.

Now add the yolks to the béchamel and mix well. In a clean stainless bowl whisk the egg-whites, fold one third into the goats cheese mixture, followed by the rest, cut up the 50g goats cheese into fine dice, fill the prepared ramekins to a third then divide the cheese between the 4, now fill with the rest of the mixture, smooth off the top, run your thumb around the edge. Put into the oven for 10 minutes. Remove from the oven, take the soufflés out of the ramekins and put into a gratin dish (this can be done hours before). When ready to eat, pour the cream into the gratin dish over the soufflés and put back into the oven for a further 10 minutes until hot and fluffy. Serve with a rocket salad.

Fillet of North Sea Halibut with Buttered Sand Hutton Asparagus, 'Bleikers' Smoked Salmon and Tartare Veloute

Andrew Pern

The Star, Harome

Andrew Pern is chef-proprietor of Michelin Star Restaurant and Egon Ronay Gastropub of the Year 2006, The Star, Harome. He specialises in traditional British style with spiced up old favourites and Anglicised classics using, wherever possible, seasonal produce from a strong network of suppliers.

See directory entry on page 90.

Recipe information

Serves: 2
Prep time: 30 minutes
Cooking time: 20 minutes

Ingredients

For the velvet crab stock:

2 x 250g Halibut Steak - skinless and boneless
8 blanched and trimmed asparagus spears
10ml olive oil
10g unsalted butter
100ml good fish stock
50ml dry white wine
5g capers
5g roughly chopped gherkins
10g roughly chopped flat parsley
10g roughly chopped dill
5g 'banana' shallot - peeled and sliced on an angle to give larger oval rings
50g cold-smoked salmon - cut into thin strips
75ml whipping cream
½ lemon juice
Seasoning

Method

In a small thick-bottomed sauce pan reduce the wine and fish stock by half, add the cream and reduce again by half.

Whilst these are reducing heat a non-stick frying pan, when hot add a drop of olive oil and a knob of butter, gently colour the asparagus spears until lightly coloured. Remove from the pan and keep warm.

Check the sauce is to required consistency, add the capers, gherkins, sliced shallots, smoked salmon and herbs. Check seasoning. Keep warm.

In the same pan as the asparagus was cooked in shallow-fry the halibut steaks, season first then lightly colour in a little butter and oil again, approx 2 minutes each side. Finish with a squeeze of lemon.

Arrange the asparagus spears onto a warmed dinner plate, place the cooked halibut on top, then spoon the sauce around and serve immediately.

Rosemary-Raisin Sponge Cake, with Honeyed Lowna Dairy Goats Cheese

John Topham
The General Tarleton

The General Tarleton is passionate about serving tasty freshly prepared food and its provenance, working with local farmers and suppliers to obtain the best quality seasonal produce – fish, game, lamb and beef, soft fruit, vegetables and farmhouse cheeses to create an innovative selection of mouth watering and visually inspiring dishes using local produce in an imaginative way.

See directory entry on page 90.

Recipe information
Cooking time: 28 minutes approx

Ingredients

Honey sauce:

150g honey
100g white wine
1 medium sized sprig of rosemary

Honeyed goat cheese:

250g fresh Lowna Dairy, Raywell goats cheese
200g cream cheese
50g sour cream
1 tsp chopped rosemary
3 tbsp finely chopped hazelnuts
2½ tbsp calvados
1½ tbsp honey
1 tsp salt
150g heavy cream
Freshly ground pepper

Rosemary-Raisin Cake:

2 tbsp good grade olive oil
300g plain flour
25g self-raising flour
1½ tsp baking powder
1½ tbsp chopped rosemary
Pinch of salt
3 eggs
275g light brown sugar
¾ tsp vanilla extract
450g raisins

Method

Combine the honey and white wine in a small saucepan and bring to the boil. Lower the heat and simmer, 3-4 minutes. Remove from the heat, add the fresh rosemary, and allow to infuse for 10 minutes. Strain, add the lemon juice, and set aside.

In a bowl of a kitchen mixer, combine the goats cheese, cream cheese, and sour cream. Cream until smooth and light, 3-4 minutes. Stir in the rosemary, hazelnuts, calvados, honey, salt and pepper to taste.

Whip the cream to soft peeks and fold into the goats cheese mix. Place a thin cloth over a colander, place the cheese mixture into the cloth and twist the cheese cloth around the cheese, flatten and place over a bowl to drain. Place in the fridge for 2 hours or overnight.

Pre heat the oven to 180°C. Lightly oil and flour a 9" cake tin.

Sift together the flours, baking powder and salt, add the chopped rosemary.

Beat the eggs and brown sugar together until well blended together, but not increased in volume. Stir in the vanilla extract and 2 tbsp of olive oil, add the egg mixture to the dry ingredients, stirring until just combined, fold in the raisins, but don't over mix else the cake will become dry.

Spread the batter evenly into the cake tin and bake for about 20 minutes until golden brown and firm to touch.

Slice the rosemary cake and serve with a spoonful of the goats cheese mix, drizzle with the honey syrup.

Apricot and Raisin Cheesecake

HARVEY NICHOLS

Richard Walton Allen

Head Chef at the Fourth Floor Café,
Harvey Nichols Leeds

Richard Walton Allen recognises the importance of using locally sourced meat, game and vegetable and was recently voted 'Best Chef 2006' with the Fourth Floor gaining 'Restaurant of the Year' at Let's Eat Leeds Association Awards.

Recipe information
Serves: 4
Cooking time: 50 minutes-1 hour

Ingredients
250g crushed digestive biscuits
125g melted butter
1lb 5oz ricotta
1lb 5oz cream cheese or marscapone
7oz Yorkshire honey
3 egg whites
3oz sugar
3 egg yolks
3½ tbsp soaked raisins
3½oz chopped dried apricots
Zest of 5 lemons
3½ tbsp Amaretto

Method
Makes 1 small deep cheesecake ring.
Mix biscuits and butter together and press into a paper lined tin.
Make the egg whites into meringue with the sugar and set aside.
Whisk together all the ingredients until smooth and then fold in the meringue.
Pour onto the lined base and bake in the oven for 50 mins-1 hour. 180°C.
Once cooked, chill until set and serve cold or at room temperature.

Yorkshire Tapas

Stephanie Moon

Clocktower at Rudding Park

See directory entry on page 170.

Clocktower combines a cosmopolitan fusion of interior design inspirations from all over the world with a menu of the finest locally sourced dishes.

Award winning executive chef Stephanie Moon designs seasonal menus around locally-sourced ingredients. Her signature dish is the Yorkshire Tapas which can be enjoyed either as a light bite or as part of a meal.

deliciouslyorkshire

Yorkshire Tapas

Deep Fried Whitby Smoked Haddock in Black Sheep Beer Batter with Real Chips and Tartar Sauce

4 goujons of smoked haddock · 1 large potato, peeled and sliced into chips · 100g self-raising flour · 100ml Black Sheep Ale · pinch of salt

To make the batter mix the flour, ale and salt together until smooth and place in the fridge until required.

Blanche the chips in cold water until soft, then place in the fryer and cook until golden and crispy.

Lightly dust the haddock goujons in a little flour, coat in the beer batter. Gently drop into the fryer and fry until golden & crispy.

Place the fish and chips into a printed newspaper cone and top with some tartar sauce.

Bleikers Smoked Salmon Parcel

1 sheet of spring roll pastry cut into 4 smaller squares · 30g sliced smoked salmon · 30g soft Yorkshire cream cheese · 4 hazelnuts · 1 tbsp plain flour mixed with 1 tbsp water to form a thick paste

Place the smoked salmon and cream cheese in the centre of each spring roll square with a whole hazelnut in the middle.

Place the square on a diagonal and fold the 2 edges to meet in the middle, fold the bottom edge into the middle and then roll to form a spring roll shape. Seal the edges with the flour and water paste.

Set in the fridge and deep fry when needed.

Mini Yorkshire Pudding with Roast Sirloin of Yorkshire Beef and Horseradish Cream

4 small slices of cooked sirloin of Yorkshire beef · 100g plain flour · 100ml milk · 2 medium eggs, beaten · oil for cooking · 1tbsp mascarpone · ½ tsp chopped chives · 1 tsp creamed horseradish

Mix together the flour, egg and milk, add a pinch of salt. Sieve the mixture and refrigerate for ½ hour. Skim the mix before use.

Pour a drop of oil into each mini Yorkshire pudding mould and place in the oven until very hot. Pour the mix into the moulds and return to a hot oven until cooked.

To make the horseradish cream, mix the mascarpone, chives and horseradish together. Add a little salt & pepper to taste.

Place a slice of the beef sirloin into each pudding and top with horseradish cream.

Holme Farm Venison with Poached Pear

2 slices of lightly smoked Holme Farm venison · 1 pear, peeled · ½ pint red wine · 2 tbsp caster sugar · ½ cinnamon stick · ½ bay leaf

Place the red wine, sugar, cinnamon stick and bay leaf in a pan and simmer over a low heat. Poach the pear in the liquid for approximately 8 minutes until cooked through and soft. Allow to cool, cut in half to remove the core and slice into small nugget shapes.

Trim the slices of venison and cut into 4 strips. Place a slice of pear onto the venison, roll and skewer with a bamboo skewer, serve cold.

Flat Mushroom with Red Onion Marmalade, glazed with Wensleydale Cheese

4 small flat mushrooms · 2 tbsp butter · 2 thinly sliced red onions · 2 tbsp brown sugar · 1 glass red wine · 1 tbsp red wine vinegar · 1 tsp chopped thyme · 100g Wensleydale cheese, grated

To make the marmalade fry the onions in ½ of the butter, add the brown sugar and caramelise. Add the vinegar, evaporate, then add the wine and reduce with the thyme. When soft remove and cool.

Peel the mushrooms, place on a tray and season. Add a small knob of butter in the centre of each and bake until soft [approx 5 minutes].

Spoon a little red onion marmalade in the centre of each mushroom, then top with the grated Wensleydale. Grill until golden and serve.

Tartlet of Sauteed Leeks with Settle Quince Jelly and Ribblesdale Goats Cheese

4 canape tartlet cases · 1 leek, washed, cut and diced · 100g Ribblesdale goats cheese, grated · 4 tsp quince jelly.

Saute the diced leeks in a little butter. Place a teaspoon of leeks into the base of the pastry case. Add a teaspoon of quince jelly on top and cover with grated cheese. Gently press the contents down into the case and then bake in the oven for 3 minutes at 180°C.

Braised Yorkshire Dales Shin Beef

Sponsored by

Yorkshire Dales Meat's award-winning traditional produce is locally reared, naturally fed, humanely slaughtered and traditionally hung.

Its own suckler herd of beef cows and calves graze the hill pastures of Reeth in Swaledale and are later fed on maize, barley and beans grown on its own farm. Calves remain with their mothers for six months enabling them to mature naturally for a distinctive quality and flavour.

Chicken, Swaledale lamb and outdoor reared Yorkshire pork all from traditional breeds available through local food shows, delis, farm shops and restaurants.

See directory entry on page 82.

Recipe information

Serves: 6
Prep time: 24 hours
Cooking time: 1-2 hours

Ingredients

2 kg Shin beef x 1 (trimmed and cubed)

2 garlic cloves (halved)
1 celery stick (cut 2" pieces)
1 carrot peeled (cut 2" pieces)
1 small onion (cut 2" dice)
1 bay leaf
2 thyme sprigs
10 white peppercorns (crushed)

600ml red wine
300ml ruby Port

750ml good beef stock
Salt & pepper (to taste)

Method

Marinade beef with vegetables, herbs and liquor for 24 hours.
Then drain and separate the beef and vegetables but be sure to keep the liquor for the sauce later. Seal the meat in a hot pan with oil until caramelised. Lift out of the pan and in the same pan seal the vegetables until golden brown, add beef and herbs to the vegetables, then add the marinating liquor and beef stock. Braise in oven until tender at 160°C for 1-2 hours. Pick out all beef and reduce liquor to desired consistency of your sauce. Strain the sauce and place the beef back in to the reduced sauce and serve, fridge or freeze.

Serve with classic mash potato and buttered vegetables.

A perfect dish to cook well in advance of your dinner party.

Recipe supplied by Boutique Catering (see entry on page 159).

Sirloin Steak Stuffed with Cropton Beer Marinated Cheese

Sponsored by

Cropton Brewery - Beer has been brewed in Cropton since 1613 and the ancient craft returned to the village in 1984 when Cropton Brewery was established in the cellars of the New Inn. The family-run inn prides itself on offering quality food and drink in the restaurant, bar and conservatory, as well as accommodation.

See directory entry on page 72.

Recipe information

Serves: 4
Prep time: 5 minutes
Cooking time: to taste

Ingredients

4 sirloin steaks (about 2 ½ cm thick)
160g/5½oz mature cheddar
4 tsp whole grain mustard
Several drops Worcester sauce
100ml beer

Method

Mix together the cheese, mustard, Worcester sauce and beer. With a sharp, pointed knife, make a lateral incision in the side of the steak. Proceed to make a pocket inside the steak and stuff the cheese mixture into it. Try to keep the entrance hole as small as possible, and the pocket as large as possible without piercing the surface or other edges of the steak. Secure the opening with half a cocktail stick that's been soaked in water – which prevents it from burning. Just before cooking, season the steak with salt and pepper, brush with oil and barbecue or char-grill until cooked to your liking.

Recipe supplied by Richard Fox (see page 32).

½ Fat Blueberry Muffins with Delyte 5

Sponsored by

Ulrick&Short

Ulrick and Short supply ingredients which are completely free from chemical, enzymic or genetic modification, specialising in ingredients for bakery, processed meats, sauces and coatings.

See directory entry on page 152.

Recipe information

Makes 12 Muffins

Cooking time: 20-30 minutes

10.8% Fat (Compared to 19.2% fat if all butter used)

Ingredients

110g/4oz plain flour
22g/¾oz Delyte 5*
55g/2oz butter
65g/2½oz caster sugar
2 eggs
1½ tsp baking powder
125g/4½oz blueberries
33ml/2 tbsp water
Pinch nutmeg

* Delyte 5 available from Ulrick & Short

Method

Cream the butter and sugar together then slowly add the eggs and water and mix for 3 minutes. Add the flour, Delyte 5, baking powder, nutmeg and mix. Slowly mix in the blueberries.

Place a spoonful of mixture into each muffin case, filling each just over half way.

Bake in an oven set at 200°C/400°F/Gas Mark 6 for 20 minutes or until golden on top.

deliciouslyorkshire

Casserole of Beef in 'Nightmare'

Sponsored by

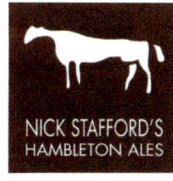

NICK STAFFORD'S HAMBLETON ALES

Recipe information

Serves: 4-6
Prep time: 30 minutes
Cooking time: 2½ hours

Ingredients

2lb (900g) braising steak cut into 2" (5 cm) squares
15fl oz (425ml) Hambleton Nightmare
1 tbsp olive oil
12oz (350g) onions, peeled and cut in quarters
2 garlic cloves, crushed
1 heaped tbsp plain flour
A few fresh thyme sprigs
2 bay leaves
Salt and freshly milled black pepper

For the croutons:

1 tbsp olive oil
1 garlic clove, crushed
6 x 1" (2½ cm) thick slices French bread cut slightly diagonally
6 level tsp wholegrain mustard
4oz (110g) grated Gruyère cheese

Hambleton Ales are brewers of real ale and bottlers of the finest quality premium ales from the heart of Yorkshire, as well as the leading British brewed gluten-free ale and lager in the world.

Beers available in pubs, off licences, supermarkets and restaurants all over the UK.

See directory entry on page 73.

Method

You will also need a large, solid baking sheet and a large, wide, flameproof casserole.

The croutons can be made in advance. Pre-heat the oven to Gas Mark 4/350°F/180°C. Drizzle the olive oil on to the baking sheet, add the crushed garlic, then, using either your hands or a piece of kitchen paper, spread the oil and garlic all over the baking sheet. Now place the bread slices on top of the oil, then turn them over so that both sides have been lightly coated with the oil. Bake for 20-25 minutes till crisp and crunchy.

To prepare the beef lower the oven temperature to Gas Mark 2/300°F/150°C. Take the flameproof casserole, place it over direct heat, then heat the oil until sizzling hot and fry the meat, 3 or 4 pieces at a time, until they turn a dark mahogany colour on all sides. Make sure you don't overcrowd the pan or they will create steam and never become brown. As you brown the meat remove it to a plate then, when all the meat is ready, add the onions to the pan, still keeping the heat high. Toss them around until they become darkly tinged at the edges – this will take about 5 minutes. After that add the crushed garlic, let that cook for about 30 seconds or so, then turn the heat down, return the meat to the casserole and sprinkle in the flour. Using a wooden spoon, stir until all the flour has been absorbed into the juices. It will look rather stodgy and unpromising at this stage but not to worry – the long slow cooking will transform its appearance.

Now gradually stir in the beer and, when it's all in, let the whole thing gently come up to simmering point, and while that's happening add salt, freshly milled black pepper and the thyme and bay leaves. Then, just as it begins to bubble, put the lid on, transfer it to the centre shelf of the oven and leave it there for 2½ hours. Don't be tempted to taste it now or halfway through the cooking as it does take 2½ hours for the beer to mellow and become a luscious sauce.

Just before you want to serve the beef, pre-heat the grill, spread the croutons with the mustard and sprinkle them with the grated Gruyère, then arrange them on top of the meat and pop the casserole under the grill until the cheese is bubbling. Then serve straight away.

Swaledale Goat's Cheese and Pancetta en Croute with Apple Chutney

Sponsored by
The Swaledale Cheese Company

Producers of the award-winning Swaledale range of cheeses, featuring the original Swaledale Ewes milk cheese (P.D.O.). Other varieties include Blue Swaledale, Swaledale with Chives and Garlic and the popular Old Peculier Cheese, which is infused with the locally brewed Old Peculier Theakston's Ale.

The cheeses are either finished with a natural rind or waxed coating. All are made with pasteurised milk, vegetarian rennet and are GM free. Today, the cheeses are handmade with dedication in the historic market town of Richmond.

See directory entry on page 70.

Recipe information
Serves: 4
Cooking time: 40 minutes approx

Ingredients

For the en croute:
2 tbsp butter
110g/4oz baby spinach leaves
Freshly grated nutmeg
Salt and freshly ground black pepper
4 slices pancetta
200g/7oz rindless soft goat's cheese log
250g/9oz puff pastry, rolled out to 5mm/¼"
1 free-range egg, beaten

For the chutney:
100g/4oz light muscovado sugar
1 shallot, finely chopped
1 tsp fresh ginger, finely chopped
1 tsp mixed spice
½ tsp dried chilli flakes
2 apples, cored and chopped
110g/4oz sultanas
60ml/2½fl oz white wine vinegar

Method

Preheat the oven to 200°C/400°F/Gas Mark 6.

For the en croute, melt the butter in a frying pan over a medium heat. Add the spinach and cook until just wilted. Add a pinch of freshly grated nutmeg and season well with salt and freshly ground black pepper. Remove from the pan and leave to cool.

Wrap the pancetta rashers around the goat's cheese. Place into the same hot frying pan and cook for 2 minutes on each side, then remove and set aside to cool.

Cut the puff pastry into two large rounds. Place the spinach into the centre of one of the pastry rounds. Top the spinach with the cooled pancetta-wrapped goat's cheese and season well with salt and freshly ground black pepper.

Brush the edge of the pastry round with the egg and place the remaining piece of pastry over the top. Press the pastry down and crimp the edges. Score the top of the pastry in a circular pattern and brush with the remaining egg wash. Place the pastry parcel onto a baking tray and transfer to the oven to bake for 20 minutes, or until golden brown and cooked through.

For the chutney, heat a pan, add the sugar and allow to melt. Add all of the remaining chutney ingredients and cook for 15-20 minutes, until the apples are tender and the chutney has thickened slightly, then remove from the heat and allow to cool.

To serve, place a half of the goat's cheese en croute onto each plate with a spoonful of chutney placed alongside.

Creme Bruleé with a Nutty Ice

Sponsored by

Northern *Select* Foods

Food wholesalers to hotels, restaurants, cafes, outside caterers, delicatessens and other retailers. Products range from fresh, chilled, frozen, through to roasted and dried goods. Delivering in the north east Monday-Friday.

We stock a wide range of cheeses, meat products, ice-cream, fruit purees, sauces, and fresh mushrooms, herbs and eggs. Our range of dried goods is extensive for example; herbs and spices, flour, sugar, nuts, tinned produce, pasta and various pastry casings, dried fruit/veg our other vegetables include roasted and frozen.

See directory entry on page 98.

Recipe information

Serves: 4
Prep time: 20 minutes
Cooking time: 40-45 minutes

Ingredients

1 packet microwave ready popcorn (salted)
6 egg yolks
600ml double cream
20g sugar
Sea salt to taste
2 sheets of rice paper

Ice cream mixture:

600ml double cream
6 egg yolks
25g sugar
½ jar peanut butter
½ vanilla pod

Method

Cook popcorn following the instructions on packet, place on baking sheet and allow to dry in the bottom of a hot oven. Mix the egg yolks, cream and sugar in a bowl but do not allow to foam. Blitz popcorn in food processor until fine powder. Add 25g popcorn powder to the egg mixture and salt to taste. Place mixture in glass ramekins and allow to rest. Bake in low to medium oven for around 40-45 minutes until just firm. Place in fridge to set.

Ice cream mixture

Whisk egg yolks and sugar in bowl until sugar dissolved. Bring cream to the boil with the vanilla pod and peanut butter. Add a little of the cream to the eggs and then add all the eggs back to the pan, reduce heat and stir constantly until custard thickens (should just coat the back of a spoon). Allow to cool. Churn in ice cream machine.

To finish

Make cones from the rice paper and fill them with popcorn powder, sprinkle brulle with a little sugar and popcorn powder, glaze with a hot lamp or hot grill until a light crisp caramel is formed.

Serve with large scoop of ice cream and garnish with the cone and rhubarb crisps.

Recipe supplied by Mr Sean Wilkinson, Head Chef, Gourmet, Durham.

Yorkshire Ruby Gold Cheese Smoked Chicken and Avocado Salad

Sponsored by

Cryer and Stott cheese mongers aim to be the premier merchant of Yorkshire cheese and produce. Cryer & Stott own three deli shops. Named in the top 15 cheese merchants by 'The Independent' newspaper. Consultant to channel 4 television. Named 'Business of the Year' by 'The Regional Food Group for Yorkshire and Humber'. Producer of Ruby Gold the worlds only rhubarb cheese, which won a gold medal at the Nantwich Cheese Awards.

See directory entry on page 160.

Recipe information

Serves: 4 as a starter portion

Ingredients

4oz Ruby Gold cheese (crumbled)
1 smoked chicken breast (shredded)
1 bag mixed salad leaves (washed)
Handful toasted pine kernels
1 avocado pear (peeled, stone removed and chopped into bite size pieces drizzled with lemon juice)
Salt and pepper to individual taste

Dressing:

2 tsp rapseed oil
1 tsp Yorkshire honey (mixed together)
1 tsp balsamic vinegar

Method

Place the salad leaves in a bowl along with shredded chicken, toasted pine kernels and avocado pear and toss together, drizzle the dressing over the leaves, place in serving bowls and top with crumbled cheese.

Serve as soon as possible and enjoy a real taste of summer!

Note: When buying avocado to check for ripeness push the top of the fruit and if hard it's not ripe and if too soft will be over ripe which will make it harder to peel and chop for the salad.

Try not to prepare the pear too much in advance due to discolouring, a little lemon juice can assist here.

Chicken Tikka in Rhubarb Mayonnaise

Sponsored by

E OLDROYD & SONS LTD

A family owned company producing and packing high quality fruit and vegetables.

The company has a high media profile, being one of the countries largest producers of rhubarb, having 5 generations experience in traditionally grown winter rhubarb. Many celebrity chefs have made visits to the Oldroyd's due to the resurgence in popularity of this traditional crop. Janet Oldroyd Hulme has become affectionally known by the media as the 'High Priestess of Rhubarb'.

The company is listed as a Rick Stein Food Hero Producer.

See directory entry on page 151.

Recipe information
Serves: 2
Prep time: 20 minutes
Cooking time: 25-30 minutes

Ingredients
1lb/400g forced rhubarb
4oz/100g sugar

Mayonnaise Ingredients:
4 heaped tbsp mayonnaise
1 heaped tbsp rhubarb or mango chutney
1 rounded tsp tikka pate
Salt and pepper
¼ cucumber finely diced
2 sticks celery finely diced
8oz/200g packet of chilled cooked chicken pieces – roughly chopped

Garnish:
1 packet watercress or mixed salad leaves
Thinly sliced red onion rings

Method

Method

Oven on 170°C/Gas Mark 5.

Wipe rhubarb and chop into 1" chunks.

Place in a large, flat dish and sprinkle on 1 tbsp of water and the sugar. Cover with foil and bake for 20-30 minutes. The rhubarb should be tender, but still retain its shape.

Reserve about 16 pieces of rhubarb, discard the juice and puree the remaining pieces.

Pile the tikka mayonnaise onto a bed of watercress or salad leaves and garnish with orange zest and thinly sliced red onion rings.

Romanov Salmon

Sponsored by

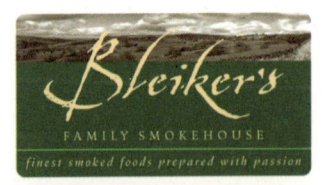

Bleiker's
FAMILY SMOKEHOUSE
finest smoked foods prepared with passion

Bleiker's gold award winning Romanov is marinated to a recipe originating from the famous deposed Russian royal family then gently cold smoked over English apple wood and free from any artificial colourings or additives. Best served with a slice of freshly buttered wholemeal bread and a squeeze of fresh lime juice accompanied by a glass of chilled unoaked Chardonnay.

See directory entry on page 75.

deliciouslyyorkshire

051

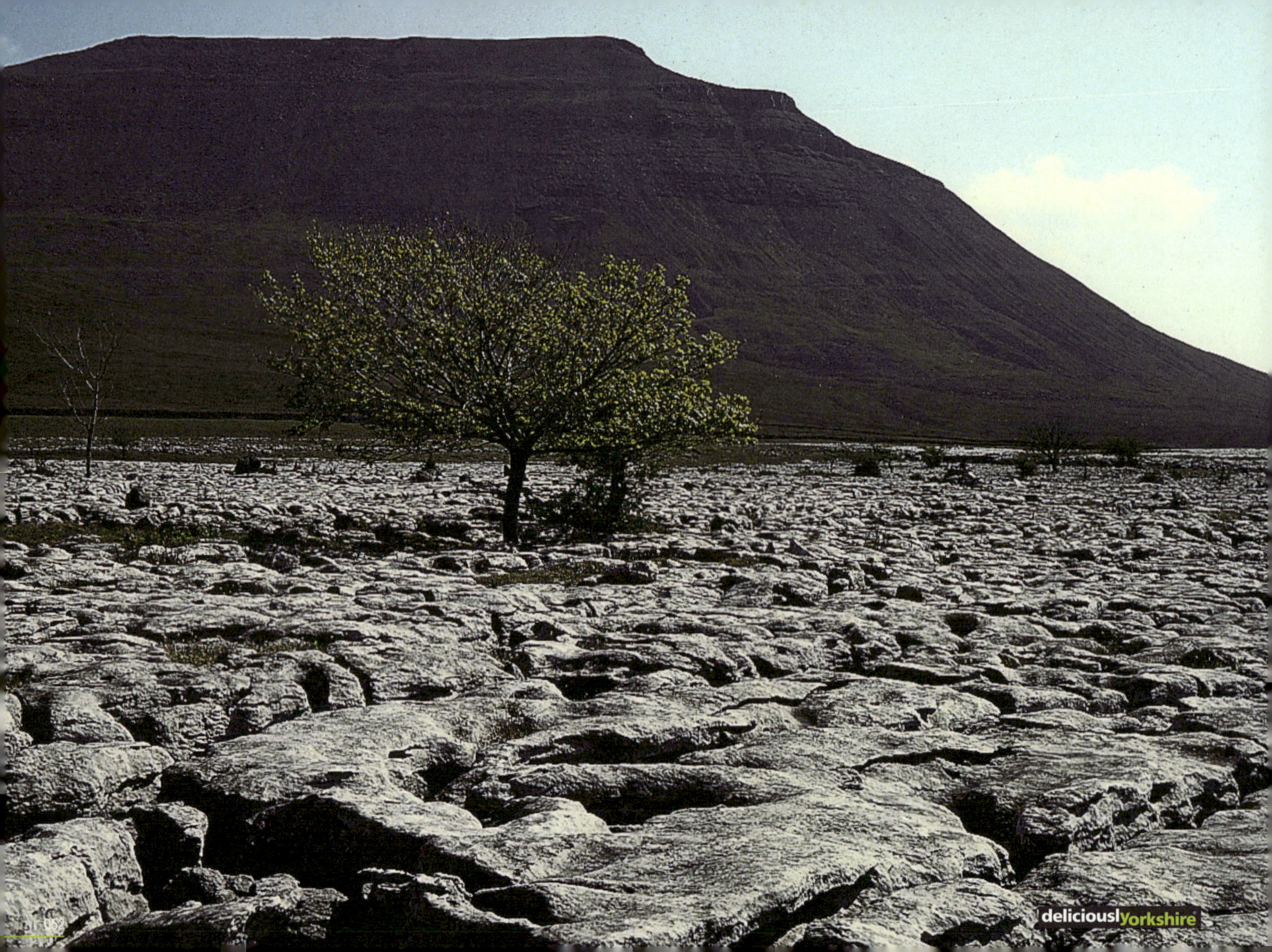

North Yorkshire

Silver grey limestone, heather-clad moors, ancient broadleaved woodlands and lush green meadows – the Yorkshire Dales offer some of the finest upland scenery in the country, making them the perfect place to enjoy, whatever the season.

The timeless landscape is marked by the distinctive network of dry stone walls that mark ancient field boundaries. Majestic scenery is the setting for picturesque villages nestling in valley bottoms and guarding centuries of history, bustling market towns, medieval cities and historic castles. In these rural communities, agriculture and food production plays a vital role in maintaining the area's economy.

Ruined abbeys (including The World Heritage Site of The National Trust-owned Fountain's Abbey), the magnificent Ripon and York Minsters, the walled city of York with its fantastic architecture and museums and annual food festivals (see Calendar of Foodie Events on page 195) are just a few of the area's attractions. Victorian floral spa town Harrogate is perfect for boutique shopping or relaxing with a glass of wine in one of the town's eateries, while the dramatic North Yorkshire coastline, which in bygone days sheltered smugglers and pirates, now provides traditional seaside holidays in picturesque fishing ports.

North Yorkshire

Leyburn 29
Northallerton 11
Hawes 32
Masham 3
Thirsk
Nidderdale
Helmsley 28 33 35
2 Pickering 27 Scarborough
19 26 20 17
Ripon 31
10 9 6 Malton
Pateley Bridge
22 4 25
30 13 18 Knaresborough 24 14
Skipton 21 12 34 23
Harrogate 5 York
15
Tadcaster
8

16 7 Whitby
1
Robin Hood's Bay

Useful contacts

www.deliciouslyorkshire.co.uk
www.visityork.org
www.yorkshire.com
www.ryedale.gov.uk
www.hambleton.gov.uk
www.moors.uk.net
www.discoveryorkshirecoast.com
www.yorkshiredales.org
www.settle.org.uk

North Yorkshire Food Highlights

deliciouslyorkshire

054

North Yorkshire Food Highlights

1. **Beacon Farm Ice Cream**
Ice cream
(see entry on p67)

2. **Beadlam Grange Farm Shop**
Farm shop & café
(see entry on p95)

3. **Black Sheep Brewery**
Visitor centre and restaurant/cafe
(see entry on p72)

4. **Colin M Robinson**
Family butcher
(see entry on p79)

5. **D.C.H**
Restaurant
(see entry on p88)

6. **Dolce Vita**
Cakes and pastries
(see entry on p65)

7. **Elizabeth Botham & Sons**
Craft bakery
(see entry on p65)

8. **English Village Salads**
Salads
(see entry on p76)

9. **Farmhouse Preserves**
Farm shop, café and PYO
(see entry on p86)

10. **Fountains Abbey & Studley Royal**
Restaurant and tea room
(see entry on p88)

11. **Lewis & Cooper**
Fine food emporium
(see entry on p92)

12. **L H Fine Foods**
Café and independent deli
(see entry on p92)

13. **Mackenzies Yorkshire Smokehouse**
Shop and restaurant
(see entry on p81)

14. **Quality Greens**
Supplier
(see entry on p98)

15. **Rafi's Spicebox**
Spice shop
(see entry on p92)

16. **Red Chard Grill Rooms**
Restaurant
(see entry on p89)

17. **Redcliffe Farm Shop & Café**
Farm shop and café
(see entry on p96)

18. **Ripley Store**
Grocer
(see entry on p93)

19. **Ryeburn of Helmsley**
Ice cream and sweet producer with shop
(see entry on p69)

20. **Seamer Fayre**
Farm shop
(see entry on p81)

21. **Swales Yorkshire Dales Ice Cream**
Ice cream
(see entry on p70)

22. **The Austwick Traddock**
Country house hotel & restaurant
(see entry on p89)

23. **The Balloon Tree Farm Shop & Café**
Farm shop & café
(see entry on p96)

24. **The Farmer's Cart**
Farm shop & café
(see entry on p96)

25. **The General Tarleton**
Bar/brasserie, restaurant and rooms
(see entry on p90)

26. **The Ginger Pig Shop**
Grocers shop
(see entry on p94)

27. **The Harmony Guest House**
Guest house
(see entry on p177)

28. **The Inn at Hawnby**
Country inn
(see entry on p90)

29. **The Little Chocolate Shop**
Visitor centre and gift shop
(see entry on p67)

30. **The Plough Inn At Wigglesworth**
Country inn
(see entry on p178)

31. **The Star Inn Speciality Foods**
Country inn
(see entry on p85)

32. **The Wensleydale Creamery**
Visitor centre
(see entry on p70)

33. **Vale of Mowbray**
Pork pies
(see entry on p83)

34. **Weeton's**
Deli
(see entry on p94)

35. **Yorkshire Cider**
Guided tours
(see entry on p75)

deliciouslyyorkshire

North Yorkshire

deliciouslyorkshire®

Shops local – Ripon and Masham

North Yorkshire has more than its fair share of pretty market towns, selling fresh, high quality produce. Here is a selection of just some of them. For a full listing of all food and drink producers in this area see pages 64 to 98 or visit www.deliciouslyorkshire.co.uk.

The area around Ripon and Masham is fertile ground for local producers. The local farming community supports a wide range of rural foodie businesses that fly the "eat local" flag. The Melmerby Business Park is home to a wealth of producers making award-winning local specialities that can be snapped up at local farmers markets and independent retailers in the area.

Local Food on Menus

Swinton Park

Swinton Park's reputation for fine food is well established, and the kitchen uses local produce and speciality foods wherever possible. Check out their Deliciouslyorkshire breakfast which uses ingredients from local suppliers including Bleiker's Smokehouse and Arthur Haigh's award winning black puddings.

Bank Villa

Bank Villa is a charming, lovingly cared for Grade II listed Georgian house, set in an acre of delightful terraced gardens. A scrumptious Deliciouslyorkshire breakfast will set you on the right "locally sourced" track.

Drink Local

Black Sheep

A traditional working brewery using time honoured methods to brew award-winning cask and bottled beer, Black Sheep Brewery has a visitor centre where you can see how the beer is brewed, have a local bite to eat in the bistro and buy some locally produced goodies from the gift shop.

Hambleton Ales

Hambleton Ales was established in 1991 in the tiny hamlet of Holme on Swale and achieved an award-winning beer within the first year. Check out their visitor's centre. Hot on the trends to innovate Hambleton Ales are brewers of the first-ever gluten-free beer, called GFA.

Local Breads
Davill's Patisserie
Davill's Patisserie is an independent master baker that produces a range of traditional breads, cakes, confectionery and chocolate, specialising in Easter eggs and premium chocolates. Café and factory demonstrations are open to the public.

Local Food
I's Pies
Anthony Sterne, recently won Waitrose small producer of the year for his unique take on a Yorkshire staple, the pie. 'Posh pies' using local ingredients to create something familiar with an unexpected twist. Flavours range from Chicken and Lemongrass to Spinach & Yorkshire Fettle, with new recipes being developed all the time.

True Foods
Andrew Mitchell makes a range of patés and sauces from honest ingredients which are used in many local restaurants.

Souper Local
Yorkshire Provender
This multi-award winning company boasts six great taste awards and has a loyal local following (look for their soups in local farm shops, Waitrose and Morrison stores). Their soups are made from fresh local produce sourced from growers in the region. Try their Yorkshire Onion Soup with Theakston's Ale for real flavour of the region.

Local Preserves
Elizabeth Smedley
Elizabeth Smedley produces award winning jams and preserves using local produce. They have their own fruit orchards in nearby Thornborough and make a wide range of chutneys, jams, marmalades pickles, mayonnaise & mustards.

Rosebud Preserves
Rosebud Preserves makes champion red onion marmalade – winning the Great Taste Award for best Yorkshire speciality. Many of their projects are made from locally sourced ingredients, including those gathered from the wild, such as elderflowers, wild crab apple and rowan berries.

North Yorkshire

Looking for Yorkshire Favourites Abroad?

Thomas Green, is a franchise of shops in Europe for customers seeking leading British (and Yorkshire!) favourites. Their headquarters is based in Ripon, assembling the best produce for expats to find on their travels.

Local Markets

Ripon

There's a market each Thursday and a farmers' market the 3rd Sunday of every month in the Market Square. Opening hours are from 9.30 am - 3 pm and a host of locally produced meat, vegetables, and specialty goods are on offer.

Masham

Market days in Masham are every Wednesday & Saturday with a wide selection of locally produced foods.

North Yorkshire

deliciouslyyorkshire®

Shops local – Thirsk

From game and hand reared pork to shellfish straight from the North Sea, the area around the northern town of Thirsk has it all.

Thirsk is nestled in between two national parks (the North Yorkshire Moors and the Yorkshire Dales), so offers stunning scenery as well as a busy racecourse and some authentic bites to eat. Pork pies, sausages and award winning cheeses are order of the day here, as well as that old fashioned Yorkshire favourite, cream tea and scones.

Local Food

Arthur Haigh Ltd

Arthur Haigh's prize-winning sausages are a real Yorkshire favourite. An unrivalled range of cooked meats, sausages and black puddings, cooked and prepared to their own traditional styles and recipes from fresh ingredients. Their famous black pudding has won numerous awards, including the Great Yorkshire Pie, Sausage and Black Pudding Competition and the Grand Prix of Black Pudding competitions, the French International Better Sausage Competition.

Hotels and Eateries

The Golden Fleece

One of the oldest Coaching Inns in England, The Golden Fleece Hotel is nearly four hundred years old and the perfect place to stay to visit the local producers in the hills out of town. A wide selection of local ales and traditional snacks are on offer in the aptly named Paddock bar and they do a locally sourced breakfast as part of the Deliciouslyorkshire scheme.

The Gallery Bed and Breakfast

Located just opposite the World of James Herriot Centre and near the market square, this B&B has a 4 diamond rating from Visit Britain. Also serves the Deliciouslyorkshire locally sourced breakfast.

North Yorkshire

Farmers' Markets

On the second Monday of the month Thirsk hosts a farmers' market, featuring the best locally produced goods. On most bank holiday Mondays the market place is filled with stalls.

On Thirsk's Doorstep/Mail Order

Shepherds Purse Cheese

Surprised by the number of patients unable to tolerate cows' milk products whilst working for an osteopath in the 80's, Judy Bell decided to experiment with ewes' milk products on her family run farm.

Thirteen years later, Mrs Bells Blue won a gold medal in the World Cheese Awards 2000, and its taste has been rated by cheese lovers as just as exquisite as a good Roquefort.

Taste Tradition

This is a mixed farm specialising in rare and traditional British breeds. From Aberdeen Angus, Hereford and Longhorn beef, to Swaledale and Suffolk lamb, to Gloucester Old Spot and Saddleback pigs, Taste Tradition can supply it. The rare breeds mature at a slower rate than commercial breeds and therefore taste better on your plate.

Peacock's Desserts

Pat Peacock brings real Yorkshire pride to freshly-made desserts. And her delicious range of mouthwatering cakes and puds are certainly the kind of home-spun good things you imagine emerging golden and fragrant from the farmhouse Aga and left to cool temptingly beside an open window. Look for her cakes at local farmers' markets and fairs.

North Yorkshire

Debbie & Andrew's Sausages

deliciouslyorkshire annual awards Winner 2006

Just a few years ago, Debbie & Andrew's sausages were a Yorkshire secret, loved by those in the know but difficult to track down. These days fans of their unique range of tasty bangers are legion.

Herbs Unlimited

Herbs Unlimited was established in 1993 by Alison Dodd as a small garden scale producer of fresh herbs to local hotels and restaurants. Her previous career as a cordon-bleu chef and restaurateur proved invaluable in understanding the catering trade requirements.

The business has grown rapidly and now also supplies much larger orders for fresh herbs from food manufacturers and wholesalers.

Yorkshire Farmhouse Eggs

Yorkshire Farmhouse Eggs is a family business that has been producing and packing the finest quality free range organic eggs for 25 years. Their chickens are kept in small flocks with daily access to fresh pasture and it is their policy to never handle intensively produced eggs.

deliciouslyYorkshire

North Yorkshire Members

Producers

Bakers and confectioners

North Yorkshire

Angel Chocolates

Melanie or Leigh Torrance   01748 884 374

The Hayloft, 1C Silver Street,
Reeth, North Yorkshire DL11 6SP

E: angel@swaledale.org
W: www.finefayre.co.uk/angel-chocolates

Fine Valrhona chocolate and wherever possible locally sourced ingredients go to make up our premium range, including fresh truffles, hand-cut slabs, bars and dipped fruits, made in the Yorkshire Dales.

Cheese & Co

Jonathan Kidd   01423 359 919

11 Centre Park, Marston Business Park,
Tockwith, York, North Yorkshire YO26 7QF

E: kidd@cheeseco.demon.co.uk
W: www.tasteofyorkshire.co.uk

Cheese has just got a new best friend with our handbaked savoury biscuits and nibbles. Oatcakes, water biscuits have never tasted this good.

Available at delis and farmshops.

Choc-Affair

Linda Barrie   07815 047 920 / 01904 541 541

Marina House, York Road, Naburn,
York, North Yorkshire YO19 4RW

F: 01904 541 541
E: linda@choc-affair.com
W: www.choc-affair.com

Choc-Affair is a producer of luxury fair trade chocolate and hot chocolate drinks.

Using only the finest ingredients, everything is made by hand to ensure chocolate of the highest quality.

We supply fine food retailers, cafes and hamper companies.

You can also purchase our chocolate from our website.

Davill's Patisserie

Ken and Shirley Davill   01765 603 544

24 Westgate, Ripon,
North Yorkshire HG4 2BQ

W: www.davills.co.uk

An accredited and award winning Independent Master Baker based in the market City of Ripon.

Produces a variety of fresh breads, delicious cakes, couverture chocolates and Easter items.

Specialises in good 'Yorkshire fayre' including Yorkshire Curd tarts, Fat Rascals and Yorkshire Parkin.

Suppliers to retailers, hotels, markets and shows.

Producers

00 see food highlight map on page 54

Bakers and confectioners

6 Dolce Vita

Sally Hudson   01653 693 343

4 Newbiggin, Malton,
North Yorkshire YO17 0JF

E: enquiries@dolcevitacakedesign.com
W: www.dolcevitacakedesign.com

Individually designed wedding, birthday & celebration cakes. Handmade danish pastries, savoury tarts, desserts, puddings and cakes. Chocolate cakes are a speciality. Natural local ingredients used. Wheat & dairy free treats always available. See website for future demonstration and course dates. Come & explore the world of Dolce Vita.

7 Elizabeth Botham & Sons

Michael Jarman   01947 602 823

35/39 Skinner St, Whitby,
North Yorkshire YO21 3AH

F: 01947 820 269
E: sales@botham.co.uk
W: www.botham.co.uk

Family run craft bakery supplying retailers and wholesalers throughout the country and abroad and pride ourselves in giving the very highest quality of product and service.

Visit our shop & award winning tearooms, or drop in to our website and browse our extensive range available for mail order.

Farrah's Harrogate Toffee

Peter Marston   01423 883 000

Camwal Road, Starbeck,
Harrogate, North Yorkshire HG1 4PY

F: 01423 883 029
E: sales@farrahs.com
W: www.farrahs.com

Farrah's original Harrogate Toffee has been made in copper pans since 1840. As well as toffee we specialise in own label gift confectionery including fudge, preserves, chocolate, nougat and rock.

It's Nut Free

Angela Russell   01609 775 660

Moxon Court, Northallerton,
North Yorkshire DL6 2NG

F: 01609 775 668
E: angie@itsnutfree.com
W: www.itsnutfree.com

Manufacturers of a range of delicious handmade products made with premium ingredients to traditional recipes and with the benefit of being nut, egg and seed free as well as being endorsed by the Vegetarian Society. Product range includes a variety of flapjacks, individual cake bars, cereal and confectionery.

Producers

Bakers and confectioners

Peacocks Desserts

Pat Peacock   01845 537 159

Leake Hall Farm, Thirsk,
North Yorkshire YO7 4BN

F: 01845 537 471
E: pat@peacocksdesserts.co.uk
W: www.peacocksdesserts.co.uk

We take real Yorkshire pride in producing the highest quality products for our customer.

Offering a range of mouth-watering, tantalizing and visually stunning cakes, pastries and desserts. Choc-a-block full of honest Yorkshire produce.

Small enough to care - big enough to deliver - whatever your needs.

Simply Chocolate

Dawn Piercy   07743 795857

10 Elm Street, Barlby, Selby,
North Yorkshire YO8 5AR

E: simplichocolate@yahoo.co.uk
W: www.simply-chocolate.co.uk

Catering and confectioners, producing home-made traditional baking using fresh locally sourced ingredients where possible, providing Chocolate fountains for any occasion and hand dipped Belgian Chocolate Truffles.

The Bakery

Sally Hudson   01653 693 343

17 Church Street, Norton,
Malton, North Yorkshire YO17 9HP

E: sally@nortonbakery.co.uk

Family run craft Bakery, producing a vast selection of standard and speciality bread and rolls, cakes and slices, fresh sandwiches and quiches. Please visit our bakery shop. Wholesale enquiries welcome.

The Chocolate Factory Ltd

Gareth East   01751 477 469

Unit 2, Hutton le Hole,
North Yorkshire YO62 6UA

E: sales@the-chocolate-factory.co.uk
W: www.the-chocolate-factory.co.uk

The Chocolate Factory produces fresh handmade chocolates, handmade chocolate figures and a full range of diabetic chocolate.

Everything made by hand with real Belgian chocolate. Watch the chocolatiers in action at The Chocolate Factory in Hutton Le Hole on the edge of the Yorkshire Moors.

Producers

00 see food highlight map on page 54

Bakers and confectioners

29 The Little Chocolate Shop Ltd

Clare Gardiner 01969 625 288

Leyburn Business Park, Harmby Road,
Leyburn, North Yorkshire DL8 5QA

F: 01969 625 027
E: info@thelittlechocolateshop.co.uk
W: www.thelittlechocolateshop.co.uk

The Little Chocolate Shop is a unique attraction in the picturesque Yorkshire Dales. Our bespoke factory includes a gift shop, a viewing area for you to watch delicious hand made chocolates and confectionery being hand crafted, and a demonstration area where you can learn about the fascinating world of chocolate.

Wharfe Valley Cheesecakes Limited

Martin Clay/Rob Neilson 07921 762 099/07894 201 936

Barker Business Park, Melmerby,
Ripon, North Yorkshire HG4 5NB

E: wharfevalleycheese@tiscali.co.uk

Manufacturers of high quality, hand crafted cheesecakes. Free from artificial colours or preservatives. We only use the finest ingredients to tantalise your tastebuds and produce a 'Dessert with a Difference'.

Woodhead Bakers Ltd

Phil Davis 01723 363 561

Beaconsfield Street, Scarborough,
North Yorkshire YO12 4EL

F: 01723 501 096
E: woodheadtb@btconnect.com
W: www.woodheadthebaker.co.uk

Family Bakers – producers of bread, sweet baked goods and meat and savoury pies. 31 retail outlets and cafes across the regions as well as through wholesalers.

Dairy and eggs

1 Beacon Farm Ice Cream

Michael or Zoe Shardlow 01947 605 212

Beacon Farm, Beacon Way, Sneaton,
Whitby, North Yorkshire YO22 5HS

F: 01947 604 670
E: beaconfarm@hotmail.com
W: www.beacon-farm.co.uk

Beacon Farm makes traditional dairy ice cream and luxury sorbets in a variety of mouthwatering flavours using fresh whole milk and double cream. We supply to the retail and catering trade and also have an ice cream parlour and tearooms here on the farm and shop selling take home packs.

North Yorkshire

deliciouslyorkshire

Producers

Dairy and eggs

Brown Eggs Ltd

Daniel Brown   01723 582 937

Redcliffe Farm, Lebberston,
Scarborough, North Yorkshire YO11 3NT

F: 01723 586 663
E: sales@browneggs.co.uk
W: www.browneggs.co.uk

Brown Eggs Ltd are producers and packers of fresh farm and free range eggs. We provide a reliable delivery service throughout North and East Yorkshire. The company is run by Mr Daniel Brown who would be delighted to speak to potential customers.

Chippindale Foods Ltd

Lorna and Nick Chippindale   01423 884 042

Kingsley Farm, Kingsley Road,
Harrogate, North Yorkshire HG1 4RF

F: 01423 885 992
E: lorna@chippindalefoods.co.uk
W: www.wheresyoursfrom.com

2007 Brit Egg Award Winner! 'Brontebrowns organic eggs' and 'Yorkshire Free Range Eggs' available in Morrisons, Booths, Brakes foodservice and wholesale food distributors across Yorkshire. Backed by the excellent website www.wheresyoursfrom.com which bridges the gap between consumers and the origins of their food, enabling people to see exactly where their eggs came from.

Payne's Dairy Ltd

Kevin Leech   01423 326 058

Bar Lane, Boroughbridge,
North Yorkshire YO51 9LU

F: 01423 325 702
E: kevin.leech@paynesdairies.co.uk
W: www.paynesdairy.co.uk

Payne's Dairies Ltd is one of the largest independent dairies in the UK.

We trade across all sectors including retail, food service, manufacturing.

We pride ourselves on quality and service producing a full range of fresh milk and creams in all pack sizes.

Producers

00 see food highlight map on page 54

Dairy and eggs

North Yorkshire

19 Ryeburn of Helmsley

David Otterburn 01439 770 331

Church Farm, Cleveland Way,
Helmsley, North Yorkshire YO62 5AT

- F: 01439 770 821
- E: info@ryeburn.com
- W: www.ryeburn.com

Ryeburn of Helmsley has been producing delicious award winning dairy ice cream and sorbet for 19 years. We have one of the largest selections of flavours in the country. We are very much a family run firm who enjoyed recognition of the quality of our products by winning numerous awards. More recently we introduced a range of handmade chocolates and chocolate figures which are also made on the premises. All the chocolates are made using Belgian chocolate, and made to the same high quality of that of our ice cream.

Shepherds Purse Cheeses Ltd

John Kerwin 01845 587 220

Leachfield Grange, Newsham,
Thirsk, North Yorkshire YO7 4DJ

- F: 01845 587 717
- E: john@shepherdspurse.co.uk
- W: www.shepherdspurse.co.uk

Shepherds Purse produces artisan award winning cheeses in our BRC higher level accredited dairy using cow's, ewe's and water buffalo milk. Our brands include Yorkshire Blue and Mrs Bell's Blue.

Crumbly

Stamfrey Farm Organics

Sue Gaudie 01609 882 297

Stamfrey Farm, West Rounton,
Northallerton, North Yorkshire DL6 2LJ

- F: 01609 882 297
- E: sue@gaudie.com
- W: www.stamfrey.co.uk

Award winning organic clotted cream, handmade using traditional methods on our own dairy farm.

Now also producing an award winning drinking/pouring yoghurt - organic of course! Ideal for breakfast over cereal or mixed with fruit to make a smoothie.

deliciouslyyorkshire

069

Producers

Dairy and eggs

00 see food highlight map on page 54

Swaledale Cheese Company

Mandy Reed 01748 824 932

Mercury Road, Gallowfields,
Richmond, North Yorkshire DL10 4TQ

F: 01748 822 219
E: sales@swaledalecheese.co.uk
W: www.swaledalecheese.co.uk

Producers of the award-winning Swaledale range of cheeses, featuring the original Swaledale Ewes milk cheese (P.D.O.). Other varieties include Blue Swaledale, Swaledale with Chives and Garlic and the popular Old Peculier Cheese, which is infused with the locally brewed Old Peculier Theakston's Ale.

The cheeses are either finished with a natural rind or waxed coating. All are made with pasteurised milk, vegetarian rennet and are GM free. Today, the cheeses are handmade with dedication in the historic market town of Richmond.

21 Swales Yorkshire Dales Ice Cream

Gary Rogers 01756 710 685

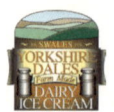

Calm Slate Farm, Halton East,
Skipton, North Yorkshire BD23 6EJ

F: 01756 710 345
E: info@yorkshiredalesicecream.co.uk
W: www.yorkshiredalesicecream.co.uk

Farm based manufacturers of genuine Yorkshire Dales ice cream, rich with fresh milk and cream, sourced directly from farms within the Yorkshire Dales National Park. Available in a variety of catering and take home packs and from our mobile fleet at Yorkshire's major visitor attractions and events.

32 The Wensleydale Creamery

Phil Jones 01969 667 664

Gayle Lane, Hawes,
North Yorkshire DL8 3RN

F: 01969 667 638
E: creamery@wensleydale.co.uk
W: www.wensleydale.co.uk

Makers of the only Real Yorkshire Wensleydale Cheese in the world. Award winning cheese, handcrafted to a time honoured recipe, using real Wensleydale milk.

Originators of delicious Real Yorkshire Wensleydale Cheese with Ocean Spray cranberries. Enjoy the 'ultimate cheese experience' at our visitor centre and view Real Yorkshire Wensleydale Cheese being handcrafted.

North Yorkshire

Producers

Dairy and eggs

Yoghurt Delights

David & Elaine Newham   01723 870 048

Highlands Farm, Burniston,
Scarborough, North Yorkshire YO13 0DL

F: 01723 871 461
E: elain.newham@btconnect.com
W: www.rfgyh.co.uk/rfg/members.asp?member_id=351

Delicious 97% fat free frozen yoghurt dessert. Low in calories. We offer the 'Healthy Alternative' to ice cream. Make your very own 'designer dessert' using vanilla frozen yoghurt. Suitable for vegetarians.

Yorkshire Farmhouse Eggs

James Potter   01845 578 376

Village Farm, Catton,
Thirsk, North Yorkshire YO7 6SQ

F: 01845 578 660
E: jamespotter@yorkshirefarmhouse.co.uk
W: www.yorkshirefarmhouse.co.uk

Yorkshire Farmhouse Eggs is a family business that has been producing and packing the finest quality free range and organic eggs for the past 25 years.

Our standards include BEIC Lion quality, RSPCA freedom foods, BRC, Soil Association, Organic Farmers & Growers and Vegetarian Society approved.

Yorvale

Lesley Buxton   01904 706 702

Fossfield Farm, Acaster Mablis,
York, North Yorkshire YO23 2XA

F: 01904 702 378
E: icecream@yorvale.co.uk
W: www.yorvale.co.uk

Award winning ice cream, fresh from the farm. Milk from Yorvale's herd of cows, locally sourced double cream and the finest carefully selected natural ingredients make this rich, creamy, indulgent ice cream.

25 flavours from the traditional vanilla to the unusual Earl Grey Tea. 8 real fruit and champagne sorbets.

Available in 120ml, 500ml, 2 litre and 5 litre tubs.

For stockist details call 01904 706 702.

Producers

Beverages – alcoholic and non alcoholic

Ampleforth Abbey

Father Rainer 01439 766 825

The Orchard, Ampleforth,
York, North Yorkshire YO62 4EN

E: rainer@ampleforth.org.uk

Our orchard, said to be the most Northern commercial orchard in England, situated in the magnificent Howardian hills has supplied apples to the local population for over 100 years. The Ampleforth monks make a variety of products including our delicious Cider.

Thirstily

3 Black Sheep Brewery

01765 689 227

Wellgarth, Masham,
Ripon, North Yorkshire HG4 4EN

F: 01765 689 746
W: www.blacksheepbrewery.co.uk

The Black Sheep Brewery visitor centre offers 'shepherded' tours of the brewery and the spacious split level bistro and baa…r provides a variety of culinary delights with beautiful views over the river Ure. The Black Sheep shop is full of 'ewe-nique' delights.

Cropton Brewery

Pauline Pilkington 01751 417 330

Woolcroft, Cropton, Pickering,
North Yorkshire YO18 8HH

F: 01751 417 582
E: info@croptonbrewery.co.uk
W: www.croptonbrewery.com

Our small, relaxed, family run inn prides itself on offering quality food, drink and accommodation, in an informal atmosphere. A choice of continental or traditional meals are served in the elegant restaurant, whilst bar meals are available in the village bar and conservatory. Beer has been brewed in Cropton since 1613. In 1984, the ancient craft of brewing returned to the village when Cropton Brewery was established in the cellars of the New Inn. Customers enjoyed the first brew of 'Two Pints' to such an extent that extra beer was produced to supply outlets further a field.

00 see food highlight map on page 54

North Yorkshire

072

deliciouslyyorkshire

Producers

Beverages – alcoholic and non alcoholic

Hambleton Ales

Nick Stafford   01765 640 108

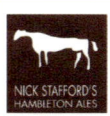

Melmerby Green Road, Melmerby,
North Yorkshire HG4 5NB

E: admin@hambletonales.co.uk
W: www.hambletonales.co.uk

Brewers of Real Ale and bottlers of the finest quality premium ales from the heart of Yorkshire available in pubs, off licences, supermarkets and restaurants all over the UK. Also the leading British brewed gluten free ale and lager in the world.

M A Worsdale

Mabel Worsdale   01677 450 276

Low Hall Farm, Hunton,
Bedale, North Yorkshire DL8 1QF

E: adamworsdale@hotmail.com

Springhill water suppliers.

Santeau

Jonathan Yates   08456 443 633

The Hydration Station, 1 Myrtle Square,
Harrogate, North Yorkshire HG1 5AR

E: info@o2go.info
W: www.wedrinkmorewater.com

You know you don't drink enough water. So, O2GO are here to help with two-calorie Flavourbursts - handy stick sachets of mineral and vitamin enhanced goodness for bottled water. Available in three fruity flavours, O2GO will help you drink more water. Mmm!

Sloe Motion

Jonathan Curtoys   0844 800 1911

Manor Farm, Eddlethorpe,
Malton, North Yorkshire YO17 9QT

E: jonathan@sloemotion.com
W: www.sloemotion.com

Sloe Motion is based on Manor Farm in North Yorkshire. All our products are handmade using hand picked wild sloes (mostly from local hedgerows). Our Sloe Gin, Whisky & Vodka are handmade in the traditional way using high concentrations of fruit to Gin ensuring fabulous flavours. We then use the Gin and Whisky infused sloes for our unique after-dinner treats, the sloe Gin or Whisky chocolate truffles. We also produce a spicy and plummy Sloe Chutney.

Producers

Beverages – alcoholic and non alcoholic

The Keld Head Springs Ltd

Michaela Hutchinson   01751 477 466

Ashgrove Farm, Marton Lane,
Pickering, North Yorkshire YO18 8LW

F: 01751 472 849
E: adamshaw-keldhead@hotmail.co.uk
W: www.keldheadspring.co.uk

Providing 100% natural Spring Water naturally raised from a Artisan well on the outskirts of Pickering.

Glass and plastic bottles in various sizes competitively priced. Small family run business providing excellent customer care.

For further information, please feel free to contact us.

The Punch Brew Co

Gregory Fildes   01744 600 981

49 Queensway, Mossbank, St Helens,
Merseyside WA11 7BY

E: enquiries@punchbrew.com
W: www.punchbrew.com / www.quiggins.co.uk

Yorkshire Herbal Punch is prepared from an olde monastic recipe, made with 12 different herbs, served warm to aid sleep, stress and anxiety, or cold to refresh as a tonic.

Thorncroft Ltd

www.thorncroftdrinks.co.uk

Sowerby Way, Eaglescliffe,
Stockton-on-Tees TS16 0RB

F: 01642 791 793
E: info@thorncroftdrinks.co.uk

Thinking about drinking? Farmshops, delis, independent retailers and large consumer shows - that's where to look for Thorncroft's unique range of plant and herb based drinks.

Traditional ingredients including hedgerow nettles and elderflowers, and innovative ingredients such as Kombucha and the extensive herbal extracts in Detox, all support our quest for health in a busy modern life. All made without preservatives, all low in sugar when diluted correctly. Or try our amazing, stylish ready to drink 'healthy thirst' range.

Producers

00 see food highlight map on page 54

Beverages – alcoholic and non alcoholic

35 Yorkshire Cider

Alex Smith   01751 417 972

Cropton, Pickering,
North Yorkshire YO18 8HH

F: 01751 417 972
E: info@yorkshirecider.co.uk
W: www.yorkshirecider.co.uk

Yorkshire Cider produces hand crafted traditional ciders and perries using locally sourced fruit. Apple juice & a range of juice mixes are also available.

Whether in bottles, bag in box or cask, delivery is throughout the Yorkshire and Humber region. For sales or guided tours contact us on 01751 417 972.

Yorkshire Country Wines

Richard & Gillian Brown   01423 711 947

Riverside Cellars, The Mill, Glasshouses,
Harrogate, North Yorkshire HG3 5QH

F: 01423 711 947
E: info@yorkshirecountrywines.co.uk
W: www.yorkshirecountrywines.co.uk

Yorkshire Country Wines produce a range of quality fruit & flower wines. Including Elderberry, Elderflower, Gooseberry, Blackberry, Damson and Rhubarb. These are not grape based and therefore each have their own distinctive taste and character.

Fish – fresh and smoked

Bleiker's Smokehouse Ltd

Charlie Andrew   01423 711 411

Glasshouses Mill, Glasshouses,
Harrogate, North Yorkshire HG3 5QH

F: 01423 712 735
E: charlie@bleikers.co.uk
W: www.bleikers.co.uk

Bleiker's Smokehouse traditionally cure & smoke a broad range of the finest quality fresh fish and authentically prepare them to the highest specifications- wherever possible free from artificial colourings, additives or preservatives. Bleiker's provenance and quality has been well recognised by the food industry. Not only have they won numerous awards for their products from the Guild of Fine Food Retailers but also continue to be one of Rick Stein's original food heroes as well as being recently selected as one of Jamie Oliver's chosen smokeries.

North Yorkshire

075

Producers

00 see food highlight map on page 54

Fresh ingredients

8 English Village Salads Ltd

Kelly Colrein 01757 617 161

Camblesforth Grange, Brigg Lane, Camblesforth,
Selby, North Yorkshire YO8 8ND

F: 01757 614 159
E: kelly.colrein@bakkavor.co.uk
W: www.bakkavor.com

For the past 16 years English Village Salads has been working with local and national growers to supply high quality produce to the UK retail market.

Our impressive local supplies include cucumber, lettuce and tomatoes, all grown to the highest quality, environmental and ethical standards.

Future Fresh Ltd

Graham Weldon 01765 640 149

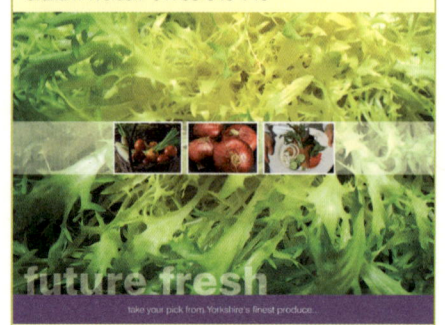

2C Melmerby Green Road, Barker Business Park,
Ripon, North Yorkshire HG4 5NB

F: 01765 640 148
E: ffsales@hotmail.co.uk

Future Fresh care passionately about Yorkshire's finest produce and we are uniquely placed to get the best from it. Our long established links with quality-led growers ensures that you'll benefit from the pick of the region's crop.

We are also committed to delivering excellence in customer service and outstanding value for money. That's why, with Future Fresh, your catering operation will be rooted in quality - it's a recipe for success all-round.

'Rooted in Yorkshire'

Herbs Unlimited

Alison Dodd 01845 587 694

Hawker Lane, Sandhutton,
Thirsk, North Yorkshire YO7 4RW

F: 01845 587 695
E: sglltd@btconnect.com
W: www.herbsunlimited.co.uk

We grow fresh cut herbs, baby salads, spinach and washed mixed lettuce freshly cut from our own farm in Yorkshire and import in winter. We specialise in unusual herbs, giving you a point of difference and often inspiration. We believe in cost effective, high quality, environmentally friendly products and we listen to our customers needs.

Producers

Fresh ingredients

J E Hartley

Tom Verity   01904 448 556

Roth Hill Lane, Thorganby,
York, North Yorkshire YO19 6DJ

F: 01904 448 479
E: tom@jehartleyfrozenveg.co.uk
W: www.jehartleyfrozenveg.co.uk

J E Hartley grows, processes, packs & freezes Yorkshire vegetables for the retail & wholesale market. Our products include delicious garden peas & petit pois, succulent carrots, parsnips & potatoes grown on our own farms.

Low Leases Organic Farm

Rob McGregor   01609 748 177

Low Street, Leeming Bar,
North Yorkshire DL7 9LU

E: info@theorganicfarm.co.uk
W: www.organicfarmfood.co.uk

Quality organic, local produce delivered for a fair price. Following expansion and co-operation with other local organic farmers, we deliver fruit & veg, meat, dairy & eggs. All produce is grown or raised by people with a passion for organic principles.

Metcalfe Organic

Mark Palmer   07801 473 619

Low House Farm, Aldborough,
Boroughbridge, North Yorkshire YO51 9HD

E: sales@metcalfeorganic.co.uk
W: www.metcalfeorganic.co.uk

Metcalfe Organic is a dedicated organic vegetable grower and packer based at Boroughbridge. We supply the carrots for the School Fruit and Vegetable scheme for Yorkshire and Humber, (240,000 pieces /week). Washed or unwashed potatoes and carrots can be supplied. Other local organic vegetables available (contact us for details). Full organic certification and Assured Produce Standards. The packing operation is NHS supplier Approved (sts certification). Products packed to order to ensure freshest quality available.

Park Lodge Farm

Trevor Fothergill   01845 577 276

Park Lodge Farm, Topcliffe,
North Yorkshire YO7 3SB

F: 05600 758 149
E: trevor@parklodgefarm.co.uk
W: www.parklodgefarm.co.uk

At Park Lodge we produce a year round supply of quality mushrooms including closed cup, flat, chestnut & portabella.

We don't use pesticides & our quality is achieved through careful choice of all influences on the final product.

We are members of the 'Assured Produce' scheme.

Producers

Fresh ingredients

Stuart's Foods Ltd

Damian & Stuart Howarth   01723 582 252

Howarth House, Dunslow Court, Eastfield,
Scarborough, North Yorkshire YO11 3XT

F: 01723 582 772
E: info@stuartsfoods.co.uk
W: www.stuartsfoods.co.uk

Sourcing, preparing and supplying only the freshest and best quality vegetables, fruits and foods for a wide range of customers locally and regionally.

We pride ourselves on our customer commitment and offering a totally bespoke service in food preparation and we are dedicated to searching out the very best specialist local produce and supporting our Yorkshire suppliers.

Ingredient suppliers

Country Products Limited

Mark Leather   01423 358 858

Unit 6 Centre Park, Tockwith,
York, North Yorkshire YO26 7QF

F: 01423 359 858
E: mark@countryproducts.co.uk
W: www.countryproducts.co.uk

From morning till night & all eats in-between,
Be it museli or porridge or a simple black bean,
Late night snacks, bite sized nibbles for a healthy routine,
We've mango & pineapple that's fit for the queen.
We've got nuts & seeds, dried fruits & savoury snacks
We supply them in bulk but most prefer our pre-packs.
We have herbs & spices to suit every cuisine
More choice & variety can rarely be seen.
For quality & value we'll never be beaten
Some say our products are the best ever eaten.

Food Design

Colin Hunter   01423 870 875

Valley House, Hornbeam Park Avenue,
Harrogate, North Yorkshire HG2 8QT

F: 01423 871 219
E: info@food-design.co.uk
W: www.food-design.co.uk

Food Design is a high quality innovative sugar ingredient manufacturer, supplying ingredients to baking, biscuit, breakfast cereal, chocolate, ice cream, chilled and frozen dessert, snack mixes.

Sweetly

Producers

00 see food highlight map on page 54

Meat, poultry and game – fresh and smoked

Arthur Haigh Ltd

Duncan Haigh   01845 578 227

Unit G Dalton Airfield Industrial Estate, Dalton,
Thirsk, North Yorkshire YO7 3HE

F: 01845 578 648
E: duncan_haigh@btconnect.com
W: www.yorkshireblackpudding.co.uk

Arthur Haigh's are based at Dalton near Thirsk, in the centre of Herriot country. We are a second-generation family business, excelling in premium award winning cooked meats and champion pork sausage varieties. We dry cure our own high quality bacon and gammon. We are black pudding Champions, winning awards both nationally and in Europe. Our speciality Doreen's Black Pudding is uniquely triangle shaped, hand made and baked. We are committed to supplying all our customers with premium goods, giving quality service and value for money.

4 Colin M Robinson

Colin Robinson   01756 752 476

Colin M. Robinson
Award Winning Family Butcher

41 Main Street, Grassington,
Skipton, North Yorkshire BD23 5AA

F: 01756 753 985
E: info@colinmrobinson.co.uk
W: www.colinmrobinson.co.uk

The premier retailer of Limestone Country traditionally bred beef. Home reared Rock View pork & lamb. Award winning home made sausages and home dry cured bacon and ham. Home made meat products and home cooked meats all prepared to the very highest of standards.

Debbie & Andrew's

Andrew Keeble   08007 836 481

Thirsk, North Yorkshire YO7 3TD

E: debbie@debbieandandrews.co.uk
W: www.debbieandandrews.co.uk

Manufacturing fresh, chilled and cooked frozen sausages on a national basis. We supply the following supermarkets: Morrisons, Asda, Sainsburys, Tesco and Budgens and offer a mail order service to those who do not have a supplier in their area.

Freshly produced food in your Locality

North Yorkshire

deliciouslyyorkshire

079

Producers

Meat, poultry and game – fresh and smoked

Holme Farmed Venison

Fiona Campbell   01977 686 440

9 First Avenue, Aviation Road,
Sherburn in Elmet, North Yorkshire LS25 6PD

F: 01977 686 441
E: fiona@hfv.co.uk
W: www.hfv.co.uk

Holme Farmed Venison provides the finest quality venison farmed to the highest standards in Yorkshire.

Our deer are naturally reared on grass pastures guaranteeing a beautifully lean and tender red meat.

We provide a wide range of cuts to restaurants, hotels, pubs, both large and small retailers and private customers.

Hornby Castle

Julia Clutterbuck   01748 811 579

Hornby Castle, Bedale,
North Yorkshire DL8 1NQ

F: 01748 812 525
E: julia@parklandrange.co.uk
W: www.hornbycastle.co.uk / www.parklandrange.co.uk

Red deer and bison graze alongside cattle in an historic eighteenth century parkland, providing low fat, low cholesterol meat high in protein and consistently tender. Free-range, grass-reared animals are high in omega-3s and cancer-fighting CLAs. Delicious flavour: healthy eating!

Contact Julia Clutterbuck for information on different cuts and venison casseroles.

Langthorne's Buffalo Produce

Paul & Kate Langthorne   01609 776 937

Crawford Grange, Brompton,
Northallerton, North Yorkshire DL6 2PD

F: 01609 776 937
E: kate.langthorne@btconnect.com

Buffalo meat, cheese and milk. Aberdeen Angus Beef, Venison, Wapiti, Wild boar, Iron age Pig, Lamb, Mutton. Collect from farm or at local farmers markets.

Speciality

deliciouslyyorkshire

Producers

00 see food highlight map on page 54

Meat, poultry and game – fresh and smoked

13 Mackenzies Yorkshire Smokehouse

Robert Crowson   01943 880 369

Units 1-6 Wood Nook Farm, Hardisty Hill,
Blubberhouses, North Yorkshire LS21 2PQ

F: 01943 880 633
E: sales@yorkshiresmokehouse.co.uk
W: www.yorkshiresmokehouse.co.uk

Set amidst the beautiful Blubberhouses Moor lies Mackenzies Yorkshire Smokehouse, a family business creating superb award winning smoked fish, meat, game and bacon. All our products plus many more from the region are available at our shop here at Blubberhouses and from our restaurant which opens in summer 2007.

Robinsons Pork Butchers Knaresborough Ltd

Mick Robinson   01423 863 077

46 Market Place, Knaresborough,
North Yorkshire HG5 8AG

E: m.wrobinson@btopenworld.com

Supply both wholesale & retail with quality pork products. Speciality pies and sausages, homemade on shop premises in the beautiful market town of Knaresborough.

Tastily

20 Seamer Fayre

Elaine Keith   01723 863 600

Bridge Farm, Main Street,
Seamer, North Yorkshire YO12 4PS

E: elaine@seamerfayre.co.uk
W: www.seamerfayre.co.uk

Seamer Fayre offers farm-to-plate meat with a travelling distance of just a few miles. Set in renovated farm buildings on the edge of Seamer village near Scarborough, our new butcher's shop sells home produced three week matured Aberdeen Angus Beef, Gloucester Old Spot pork and bacon, and lamb from our prize winning flock of Berrichou du Cher sheep raised on Stewardship land. Wild roe venison also features when in season. Banquet roasts, and joints for family and grand occasions are a speciality. The shop is currently open Wednesdays, Fridays and Saturdays 10am- 4pm

North Yorkshire

deliciouslyyorkshire

Producers

Meat, poultry and game – fresh and smoked

Taste Tradition Ltd

Joyce and Charles Ashbridge 01845 525 330

Units I & J Lumley Close, Thirsk Industrial Park, Thirsk YO7 3TD
Mount Grace Farm, Cold Kirby, Thirsk YO7 2HL

- F: 01845 525 331
- E: info@tastetradition.co.uk
- W: www.tastetradition.co.uk

Taste Tradition is a family run business producing and supplying the highest quality rare/native breed meat.

Our pork, lamb and beef are served in some of the finest restaurants, stores and butchers nationwide.

Our breeds include Gloucester Old Spot, Saddleback, Welsh Pork, Longhorn, Galloway and Dexter Beef, Swaledale and Suffolk Lamb.

Specialities - suckling pig, porchetta and sausages.

Whole Hog Sausage Company

Peter Olley 01765 690 680

Unit 3D Sycamore Business Park, Dishforth Road,
Copt Hewick, Ripon, North Yorkshire HG4 5DF

- E: po@properstuff.com
- W: www.wholehogsausage.co.uk

All the prime cuts of free range Yorkshire pork in a sausage! Served by leading chefs: General Tarleton, Ferrensby. Devonshire, Bolton Abbey. Angel, Hetton. Deanery, Ripon.

Yorkshire Dales Meat Company

Stephen Knox 01748 810 042

Mill Close, Patrick Brompton, Bedale,
North Yorkshire DL8 1JY

- F: 01748 813 612
- E: info@yorkshiredalesmeat.com
- W: www.yorkshiredalesmeat.com

Suppliers of excellent quality Beef, Pork, Lamb and Poultry all sourced in Yorkshire using traditional breeds. Quality and maturation paramount. We supply top quality restaurants throughout the Yorkshire and Humberside area and our ever expanding customer base includes top London restaurants. We supply Londis and Costcutter with our range also many delis, farm shops and selected outlets.

Superbly

Producers

00 see food highlight map on page 54

Meat, poultry and game – fresh and smoked

Yorkshire Game Ltd

Richard Townsend 01748 810 212

Station Road Industrial Park, Brompton-on-Swale, Richmond, North Yorkshire DL10 7SN

F: 01748 810 228
E: sales@yorkshiregame.co.uk
W: www.yorkshiregame.co.uk

Yorkshire Game supplies fresh oven ready game and specialist foods to the catering trade, operating from an EC export licensed plant in North Yorkshire. Wild Scottish Venison, Grouse, Pheasant, Partridge, Wild Duck, Woodpigeon, Hare and Rabbit are our most popular products. We supply specialist foods to wholesalers, butchers and chefs in the North of England.

"The Ivy uses Yorkshire Game because we use only the best seasonal British produce" - Mark Hix, Chef Director, The Ivy, London.

Pies

Independent Foods (I's Pies)

Anthony Sterne 01765 641 200

Barugh Close, Barker Business Park, Melmerby, Ripon, North Yorkshire HG4 5NB

F: 01765 641 201
E: info@independentfoods.co.uk
W: www.independentfoods.co.uk

Perfect pastry - makers of gourmet pies, parcels, sweet & savoury tarts.

Pastry also available in blocks or ready formed.

Deliciously

33 Vale of Mowbray Ltd

Paul Keeton 01677 422 661

5-6 Mowbray Terrace, Leeming Bar, North Yorkshire DL7 9BL

F: 01677 424 986
E: paulkeeton@valeofmowbray.co.uk
W: www.valeofmowbray.co.uk

Vale of Mowbray have been producing famous pork pies in Leeming Bar, North Yorkshire, since 1928. During this time the recipe has been perfected to offer our customers a rich crispy baked pastry, filled with succulent cured meat, producing a 'flavour to savour'. There are sizes to suit everyone, from mini pork pies to slicing pies for the delicatessen. National distribution has been achieved through the multiple retailers, with a van-sales service available to the independent trade in the north of England. The van-sales service also offers a wide range of bacon, sausages and cooked meat products.

Producers

Pies

Voakes Pies

Andrew or James Voakes   01423 339 988

Whixley Grange, Whixley,
York, North Yorkshire YO26 8AY

- **F:** 01423 339 988
- **E:** enquiries@voakespies.co.uk
- **W:** www.voakespies.co.uk

Voakes Pies produce award winning pork pies.

These are made at our purpose built factory at Whixley Grange Farm, using pork from our own herd of pigs, using only the best quality ingredients. We take great care in producing a delicious pork pie for all food lovers who appreciate a quality product.

Prepared food

Bare Earth Ltd

Gary Quinn   01765 641 824

8 Hallikeld Close, Barker Business Park,
Melmerby, North Yorkshire HG4 5GZ

- **F:** 01765 641 628
- **E:** info@bare-earth.co.uk
- **W:** www.bare-earth.co.uk

A taste of Africa made in Yorkshire - Bare Earth manufactures a range of meat products - using traditional Southern African recipes.

Our core products - Biltong and Droewors, are speciality meat snacks made from cured and air dried beef, whilst Boerewors, a 100% meat sausage is gluten free, prefect for barbecuing!

The Salad Garden (York) Ltd

Mark Hawley   01904 608 848

Unit G10, Elvington Industrial Estate, Elvington,
York, North Yorkshire YO41 4AR

- **F:** 01904 608 113
- **E:** markhawley@salad-garden.com
- **W:** www.thesaladgarden.co.uk

The Salad Garden gathers ingredients selected for consistent quality in appearance, texture and flavour - the essential elements for producing premium quality sandwich fillers and compound salads.

We continue to invest in our purpose built factory and our quality systems to ensure that we maintain our high levels of hygiene and our BRC global standard food accreditation.

Producers

00 see food highlight map on page 54

Prepared food

31 The Star Inn Speciality Foods

Justin Brosenitz 01439 770 397

Harome, Nr. Helmsley,
North Yorkshire YO62 5JE

F: 01439 771 833
E: justin@starinnfoods.co.uk
W: www.starinnspecialityfoods.co.uk

Star Inn Speciality Foods has been set up by Andrew Pern and Justin Brosenitz (Old College Buddy's) which is the sister company of the renowned Star Inn at Harome.

From the kitchen's of the Star we intend to create a number of different ranges of speciality foods using only the very best of local ingredients. We will be starting with our range of exquisite Speciality sauces that will enhance any meal, and can be enjoyed in the comfort of your own home.

The Yorkshire Provender

Terry Williams 01765 641 920

5E Keld Close, Barker Business Park,
Melmerby, North Yorkshire HG4 5NB

F: 01765 641 929
E: info@yorkshireprovender.co.uk
W: www.theyorkshireprovender.co.uk

We deviate from the norm with our recipes - daring to go where no soup manufacturer has gone before. And the combinations really work.

We use as much fresh regional produce as possible and work with the seasons to achieve this.

The product is therefore essentially about provenance, quality, innovation and vibrancy.

True Foods

Mitch Mitchell 01765 640 927

Unit 5 Barugh Close, Barker Business Park,
Melmerby, North Yorkshire HG4 5NB
E: mitch@truefoodsltd.com

TRUEfoods specialises in the production of fresh stocks, sauces, pates & terrines, using the freshest local ingredients to make 100% natural products, based on culinary principles.

Regionally

North Yorkshire

deliciouslyorkshire

085

Producers

00 see food highlight map on page 54

Preserves, honey, condiments and spices

Elizabeth Smedley Speciality Foods

Chris Smedley-Nugent   01765 640 680

Melmerby, Ripon,
North Yorkshire HG4 5NB

F: 01765 641 868
E: jams@elizabethsmedley.com
W: www.elizabethsmedley.com

Elizabeth Smedley is Yorkshire based & dedicated to producing the finest, award winning, handmade preserves, produced with the finest ingredients. Our range includes jams, marmalades, chutneys, pickles, mayonnaises and mustards. Our preserves are additive and gluten free, and as we produce up to 180 different products, our range is enjoyed by a wide audience, both young and old. Our preserves are available through independent retail outlets and the National Trust, with a strict policy not to supply supermarkets or convenience stores.

9 Farmhouse Preserves

Richard Williams   01347 889 241

Mill Green Farm, Crayke,
North Yorkshire YO61 4TT

F: 01347 889 243
E: info@farmhousepreserves.co.uk
W: www.farmhousepreserves.co.uk

Farmhouse Preserves is the ultimate destination point. Visit our Café bistro for coffee or 3 course lunch - Food boutique - Pick your own vegetable patch - herb garden - Cut flower beds - award winning 'Jam workshop' - estate walk by the river . . . dogs & children welcome with well behaved Mums and Dads!

Raydale Preserves

R.D. Kettlewell   01969 650 233

School House Farm, Stalling Busk,
Leyburn, North Yorkshire DL8 3DH

F: 01969 650 233
E: kraydale@aol.com

We produce a large range of hand made chutneys, jams, jellies, curds & cakes on our farm in the heart of the Yorkshire Dales. We use local ingredients wherever possible.

Skilfully

deliciouslyorkshire

Producers

Preserves, honey, condiments and spices

Rosebud Preserves

Elspeth Biltoft   01765 689 174

Healey, Masham,
North Yorkshire HG4 4LH

F: 01765 689 174
E: elspeth@rosebud.fsworld

Manufacturer of jams, marmalades, jellies, chutneys, lemon curd, mincemeat and mustard since 1989.

Rosebud Preserves makes a range of over fifty products, principally by hand and in small batches, without the addition of additives, preservatives or colourings, using the best available ingredients (some organic) bought and gathered locally whenever possible.

White Rose Preserves

Helen & Jonathan Sunter   01969 624 806

Hill Top Farm, Moor Road,
Leyburn, North Yorkshire DL8 5DJ

F: 01969 623 565
E: info@whiterosepreserves.co.uk
W: www.whiterosepreserves.co.uk

White Rose Preserves Company produces natural marmalades, chutneys, dessert toppings and preserves on our family farm in Leyburn, Wensleydale.

Our award winning products are created using the finest natural ingredients and crafting in small batches to achieve unsurpassed rich natural colour and taste, free from artificial colours and preservatives.

Hospitality

Hotels and restaurants

Bettys & Taylors of Harrogate

Steve Evans   01423 814 000

Pagoda House, Plumpton Park,
Harrogate, North Yorkshire HG2 7LD

F: 01423 814 001
W: www.bettysandtaylors.co.uk

There are 6 Bettys Café Tea rooms to explore: the spa town of Harrogate has two branches as does York, you'll also find Bettys in Northallerton and Ilkley. All our cakes, breads and chocolates - more than 600 lines - are made by hand at our Craft Bakery, and our extensive range of teas and coffees are selected by our sister company, Taylors of Harrogate. For more information visit www.bettysandtaylors.co.uk

North Yorkshire

deliciouslyorkshire

Hospitality

00 see food highlight map on page 54

Hotels and restaurants

5 D.C.H & The Court Café-Bistro & Bar

David Brooks 01904 625 082

D.C.H

Duncombe Place, York,
North Yorkshire YO1 7EF

- F: 01904 620 305
- E: sales@deancourt-york.co.uk
- W: www.goodfoodyork.co.uk

D.C.H, has reaped awards from 2 AA Rosettes, and received excellent reviews in the Metro, Times and Independent. Décor is cool and contemporary with views of York Minster. Andrew Bingham, head chef creates menus, full fresh local produce with interesting flavours and innovative twists. Try 'The Court' our new café-bistro & bar.

10 Fountains Abbey & Studley Royal

Chris Fowler 01765 608 888

THE NATIONAL TRUST

Estate Office, Ripon,
North Yorkshire HG4 3DY

- F: 01765 601 002
- E: fountainsenquiries@nationaltrust.org.uk
- W: www.nationaltrust.org.uk

At Fountains Abbey & Studley Royal it is our aim to offer food that is healthy, delicious and sourced and prepared to the highest standards in our Restaurant and Tea Room.

We encourage the use of seasonal produce, favour high quality local suppliers and use organic produce wherever possible.

Café Harlequin

Marie Howell 01904 630 631

2 Kings Square, York,
North Yorkshire YO1 8BH

- E: marie@cafeharlequin.talktalkbusinesshosting.co.uk
- W: www.cafeharlequin.talktalkbusinesshosting.co.uk

Family run coffee and tea house committed to using quality ingredients and local suppliers.

Our menu includes sandwiches, salads, light snacks and home-made scones and cakes.

Greens

Rob Green 01947 600 284

13 Bridge Street, Whitby,
North Yorkshire YO22 4BG

- E: info@greensofwhitby.com
- W: www.greensofwhitby.com

Greens prides themselves on sourcing and using the finest of local produce, whether it be fresh turbot from Whitby quay or Yorkshire lamb from Ryedale. We are committed to serving you the best quality of Yorkshire produce available.

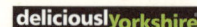

Hospitality

00 see food highlight map on page 54

Hotels and restaurants

North Yorkshire

16 Red Chard Grill Rooms

Matthew Smith   01947 606 660

22/23 Flowergate, Whitby,
North Yorkshire YO21 3BA

E: info@redchard.com
W: www.redchard.com

Contemporary style dining room offers a relaxed atmosphere for morning coffee, glass of wine and a chat with friends. Open Tuesday - Friday lunch and dinner, Saturday from 6pm and Sunday brunch or lunch till 4.30pm. Grill menu with prime Yorkshire beef and lamb, seafood specials, vegetarian dishes and homemade puds.

Spindleberry Inns

David Parker   01748 833 214

Kitchener Road, Catterick Garrison,
Richmond, North Yorkshire DL9 4HE

F: 01748 835 057
E: david@spindleberryinns.co.uk
W: www.spindleberryinns.co.uk

Our company operates three Public Houses, two being late licensed and the other is a bar/60 seater restaurant called The Blacksmiths Arms.

Situated in the attractive, secluded village of North Cowton (nr Richmond), North Yorkshire, just off the A1, on the B1263. The Blacksmiths Arms offers high quality local produce from an extensive a la carte menu.

22 The Austwick Traddock

Jane & Bruce Reynolds   01524 251 224

Austwick,
Via Lancaster LA2 8BY

E: info@austwicktraddock.co.uk
W: www.austwicktraddock.co.uk

Open minded as to what makes a fine meal, The Austwick Traddock's award winning restaurant uses local and seasonal ingredients, organic whenever possible.

Our rooms are individually designed with most enjoying impressive views of the surrounding Dales. There is also ample parking in the grounds of the hotel.

deliciouslyyorkshire

Hospitality

00 see food highlight map on page 54

Hotels and restaurants

---

25 The General Tarleton

John Topham 01423 340 284

Ferrensby, Knaresbrough,
North Yorkshire HG5 0PZ

F: 01423 340 288
E: gti@generaltarleton.co.uk
W: www.generaltarleton.co.uk

The General Tarleton - Bar/Brasserie, Restaurant and Rooms - Serving food with Yorkshire roots - AA 5 Star Accommodation, 2 Rosettes for food, Michelin Bib Gourmand. We take great care in sourcing the best local, seasonal produce available from farmers and producers who care as passionately as we do about food.

---

28 The Inn at Hawnby

Dave & Kathryn Young 01439 798 202

Hawnby, Near Helmsley,
North Yorkshire YO62 5QS

E: info@innathawnby.co.uk
W: www.innathawnby.co.uk

Shh…don't tell anyone! It's small - but special. This delightful country Inn is perched at the top of the hill in the peaceful village of Hawnby, with stunning panoramic views of the North Yorkshire Moors. Stay in the more traditional main house in one of our comfortable en-suite bedrooms, or enjoy the privacy of the converted stables, decorated in a more contemporary style. Whether it's a long lunch or a lazy weekend - The Inn at Hawnby is just perfect.

The Star Inn

Andrew Pern 01439 770 397

Harome, Nr. Helmsley,
North Yorkshire YO62 5JE

E: jpern@thestarinnatharome.co.uk
W: www.thestarinnatharome.co.uk

The small relaxed restaurant glows with the bonhomie of a proper old fashioned auberge – run with style!! Unpretentious, good hearted genius on every plate – "adore every second of being there!"

Hospitality
Great places to eat in and stay

delicious**yorkshire**

Hospitality

Outside caterers

At Home
Diana Naish   01904 709 988

The Chantry, Chantry Lane, Bishopthorpe,
York, North Yorkshire YO23 2QF

F: 01904 701 412
E: diananaish@athomecatering.freeserve.co.uk
W: www.diananaish.co.uk

York's top caterer and event organiser. Historic venues in York and beyond or your own site or marquee. Private and business functions from weddings, dinners, conferences to BBQ's, Hog Roasts and Medieval banquets.

Retailers

Deli and independent grocers

De'Clare
Clare Prowse   01904 644 410

5 Lendal, York,
North Yorkshire YO1 8AQ

E: clare.prowse@declaredeli.co.uk

We specialise in selling the very best local produce. Yorkshire Dales meats, Shepherds Purse cheeses, Holme farmed venison, Mackenzie's smoked fish and Ryedale chocolates are just a few of the many specialist foods on sale in our deli opposite the Museum Gardens along with great cakes, breads and regional Spanish and Italian food.

Carricks Fish Ltd
Nicola / Chris Revis   01677 470 499

Yew Tree House, Snape,
Bedale, North Yorkshire DL8 2TJ

E: carricks-ltd@btconnect.com

Carricks Fish Ltd is a family run business specialising in traditional and natural smoked fish, fresh fish, fresh fruit and vegetables and delicatessen.

Henshelwoods Delicatessen
Ali Vincent   01904 673 877

10 Newgate, York,
North Yorkshire YO1 7LA

F: 01904 653 845
E: info@deliyork.co.uk
W: www.deliyork.co.uk

Overlooking York's daily market Kirk & Ali Vincent source the finest and freshest local and seasonal produce to go into their daily specialities and search out the very best ingredients and delicacies from around the world to fill this little corner of foodie heaven.

Retailers

Deli and independent grocers

North Yorkshire

---

11 Lewis & Cooper Ltd

Victoria Kaye   01609 772 880

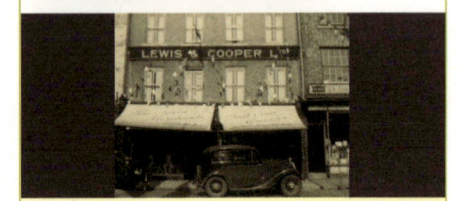

92 High Street, Northallerton,
North Yorkshire DL7 8PP

F: 01609 777 933
E: sales@lewisandcooper.co.uk
W: www.lewisandcooper.co.uk

In 1899 Mr Lewis and Mr Cooper first began offering their fine wares in Northallerton. Lewis and Cooper today is an internationally renowned gourmet store, yet remains a family business. Explore the nooks and crannies of this award winning emporium and you'll discover literally thousands of rare treats, amongst them, their handmade plum puddings generously laced with Hennessey Cognac. Manufactured by hand to a secret century-old recipe and packed with succulent fruits, they're Gold Great Taste Award winners and a definite number 1 foodie treat.

---

12 L H Fine Foods

Lucinda Hyman   01423 506 400

135 Otley Road, Harrogate,
North Yorkshire HG2 0AG

E: info@lucindahyman.co.uk

Great Taste Award winning products. Once tasted never forgotten canapes, soups, savoury tarts, delicious ready made meals, desserts, cakes, bread and sandwiches.

In house menu with coffee available all day - Quality products, prepared daily in our kitchen providing additive free, healthy food from locally sourced ingredients.

---

15 Rafi's Spicebox

Kevin Fernandez   01904 638 119

17 Goodramgate, York,
North Yorkshire YO1 7LW

E: info@spicebox.co.uk
W: www.spicebox.co.uk

Rafi's Spicebox specialise in preparing the unique 'Curry Pack', which was invented by our founder and author Rafi Fernandez. Choose from 27 varieties and spices, garlic, chillies and onions are carefully blended to your taste. Simple, no chopping and no oil. You can create an authentic curry in 25 minutes!

---

deliciouslyyorkshire

Retailers

00 see food highlight map on page 54

Deli and independent grocers

Proudfoot Group

Valerie Aston 01723 585 960

Blinking Sike, Caxton Way,
Scarborough, North Yorkshire YO11 3YT
F: 01723 585 959
E: valerie@proudfootgroup.com

Family owned regional grocery retailer. 5 stores ranging from 3,000 to 18,000 sq.ft based in Scarborough. Started by Wilf Proudfoot just after the war, now run by sons Mark and Ian Proudfoot.

18 Ripley Store

David Thomson 01423 770 044

Beechwood, Ripley,
Harrogate, North Yorkshire HG3 3AX
E: rev_22_2@hotmail.com
W: www.ripleystore.com

Serving you the finest Yorkshire produce since 1832. Set in the heart of the beautiful North Yorkshire village of Ripley.

We source the finest local foods and condiments from across our county; cakes and tarts, a superb array of pies, Yorkshire cheese, freshly baked bread, jams, preserves, vegetables, fine wine and beer.

Tarts and Titbits

Phil Black 01904 613 875

78-80 Gillygate, York,
North Yorkshire YO31 7EQ
E: phil2005black1@yahoo.co.uk
W: www.tartsandtitbits.co.uk

Small independent retailer, supplying some of Yorkshire's finest produce to a wider market. In house catering, bespoke party food and a growing range of sourced rural produce with a high level of service.

Ripley Ice Cream

David Thomson 01423 770 044

Beechwood, Ripley,
Harrogate, North Yorkshire HG3 3AX
E: rev_22_2@hotmail.com
W: www.ripleystore.com

World Famous Ripley Ice Cream. Our world famous delicious creamy tasty ice cream has been made for decades to a well kept secret recipe. With a different flavour to choose every week it will keep you coming back time and time again. Quite possibly the Best Ice Cream you will ever taste !

Healthily

North Yorkshire

Retailers

00 see food highlight map on page 54

Deli and independent grocers

26 The Ginger Pig Shop

Lisa Fraser   01751 477 211

11 Market Place, Pickering,
North Yorkshire YO18 7AA

F: 01751 474 448
E: thegingerpig1@btconnect.com

Step inside the new Ginger Pig Shop in Pickering and you will discover a traditional grocers shop. Packed full of the award winning 'Ginger Pig' meat produce, which is farmed on 1,600 acres of farmland in Levisham. Or why not try some of the freshly prepared food from the kitchens of The White Swan Inn.

34 Weeton's

Andrew Loftus   01423 507 100

23/24 West Park,
Harrogate, North Yorkshire HG1 1BJ

E: info@weetons.com
W: www.weetons.com

Over 3000 square feet dedicated to the finest and freshest Yorkshire produce. You can watch the butchers and bakers at work in this state-of-the-art farm shop, listed by The Express newspaper as one of the "Top 100 shops in the world". The bustling café is also a popular meeting place.

Yorkshire Dales Cheese Company

Jane Taylor/David Harris   01325 243 985

87 Swaledale Avenue,
Darlington, North Yorkshire DL3 9AR

E: info@yorkshiredalescheese.co.uk
W: www.yorkshiredalescheese.co.uk

If you are searching for something uniquely cheesy then look no further. The Yorkshire Dales Cheese Company, specialist suppliers of Real Wensleydale Cheese from Hawes can oblige with anything from a wedge of your favourite Wensleydale to cheese themed hampers, cheese buffets and cheese wedding cakes. For more information on how to visit us virtually or in person contact us on 01325 243 985 or info@yorkshiredalescheese.co.uk

Retailers

00 see food highlight map on page 54

Farm shops

Ainsty Farm Shop

Sam Blacker   01423 331 897

The Farm Shop, York Road, Green Hammerton,
York, North Yorkshire YO26 8EQ

F: 01423 331 897
E: info@ainstyfarmshop.co.uk
W: www.anistyfarmshop.co.uk

Farm shop with in-house butchery, selling quality local beef, pork, lamb, poultry and game.

The shop also houses a bakery, producing a wide range of breads and pastries, an extensive deli, with local cheeses, dairy products, ice creams, smoked products and a full range of locally produced preserves, along with a coffee shop.

2 Beadlam Grange Farm Shop & Tearoom

Jenny Rooke   01439 770 303

Beadlam Grange, Pockley,
York, North Yorkshire YO62 7TD

E: info@beadlamgrange.co.uk
W: www.beadlamgrange.co.uk

Newly opened in June 2007 Beadlam Grange Farmshop & Tearoom is located in lovely surroundings in our charming converted granary and old wheelhouse.

In the Farmshop customers can purchase fresh meat, fruit, vegetables, bread, cakes, preserves and much more, direct from the farm and local producers. In the delightful tearoom the menu makes good use of the produce in the shop serving traditional farmhouse fayre, light lunches and home baking.

Castle Howard Farm Shop

Rachel Jack   01653 648 444

Castle Howard, York,
North Yorkshire YO60 7DA

F: 01653 648 529
E: house@castlehoward.co.uk
W: www.castlehoward.co.uk

A delectable array of local and estate produce. A traditional butcher's counter is the focal point of the shop, accompanied by a superb deli counter, with a range of seasonal fruit and vegetables plus fresh bread, dairy products and beverages and preserves. Admission to farm shop, plant centre, gift shops and cafes is free.

Retailers

00 see food highlight map on page 54

Farm shops

17 Redcliffe Farm Shop and Café

Martin Brown   01723 583 194

Redcliffe Lane, Lebberston,
Scarborough, North Yorkshire YO11 3NT

F: 01723 583 194
E: office@redcliffefarmshop.co.uk
W: www.redcliffefarmshop.co.uk

Our deli-style farm shop offers a comprehensive selection of fresh meat, seasonal vegetables, eggs, dairy, Yorkshire cheeses, ice cream and locally made preserves. We produce home baked delicacies, pies and quiches. After shopping you can enjoy lunch, or coffee and a cake in our café, everything is made on the premises.

23 The Balloon Tree Farm Shop & Café

Julia Roe   01759 373 023

Stamford Bridge Road, Gate Helmsley,
York, North Yorkshire YO41 1NB

F: 01759 373 644
E: info@theballoontree.co.uk
W: www.theballoontree.co.uk

Award winning farmshop, specialising in rare breed meats and 'superfresh' homegrown fruit and vegetables harvested daily (by superfresh we mean minutes and hours old, not days!) Both shop and cafe offer the finest homemade food including quiches, scones, cooked hams and beef, scotch eggs and award winning cakes and chutneys. Landscaped cafe garden. PYO in the summer months.

24 The Farmer's Cart

Edward Sykes   01904 499 183

Towthorpe Grange, Towthorpe Moor Lane,
York, North Yorkshire YO32 9ST

F: 01904 491 918
E: info@thefarmerscart.co.uk
W: www.thefarmerscart.co.uk

At the Farmer's Cart we pride ourselves on our freshly picked and home-grown fruits and vegetables; served in our farm shop and restaurant. The farm's traditionally reared Aberdeen Angus beef, rare breed pork and lamb supply our newly opened butchery counter. Our award-winning delicatessen offers an array of Yorkshire cheeses, homemade salads and quiches. Seasonal family activities and school tours. Regional Food Group Yorkshire & Humber Farm Shop of the Year 2006.

Retailers

Farm shops

The Forge Farm Shop & Sandwich Bar

Judith Wolloms, Fiona Peacock & Lynne Robertson 01765 698 249

The Old Smithy, Canal Wharf, Bondgate Green,
Ripon, North Yorkshire HG4 1AQ
E: cw@freemantleplace.fsnet.co.uk

The Forge is a farm shop and sandwich bar that offers customers a tasty choice of freshly-made sandwiches, local farm produce, and home made cakes, soups, salads etc.

Organically

The Organic Pantry

Fanny Watson 01937 531 693

St Helens Farm, Newton Kyme,
Tadcaster, North Yorkshire LS24 9LY
F: 01937 834 062
E: office@theorganicpantry.co.uk
W: www.theorganicpantry.co.uk

The Organic Pantry is a family run organic farm based at Newton Kyme, growing over 50 different varieties of organic vegetables which we sell via our comprehensive box scheme/delivery service, farm shop and website.

We supply other outlets/shops/restaurants through our wholesale business, but NO supermarkets.

Distributors

Ackroyds Restaurant Meats

Stuart Ackroyd 01904 728 217

Carp Lake, Crockey Hill,
York, North Yorkshire YO19 4SR
F: 01904 728 231
E: stuart@ackroydsmeats.co.uk
W: www.ackroydsmeats.co.uk

Supplying a full range of locally sourced fresh British meats and poultry to caterers since 1977.

Ackroyds Restaurant Meats operate a regional delivery service from purpose built premises near York.

Freshly

North Yorkshire

Distributors

00 see food highlight map on page 54

14 Quality Greens

Angela Bailey   01904 468 029

Gravel Pit Farm, Sand Hutton,
York, North Yorkshire YO41 1LN

F: 01904 468 028
E: enq@qualitygreens.co.uk
W: www.qualitygreens.co.uk

Quality Greens Limited, is dedicated to the highest standard of fresh fruit and vegetable produce including prepared produce that is supplied shrink-wrapped and ready to cook. Customers include high quality restaurants and schools. Customers may choose to collect or have produce delivered. Suppliers include local growers.

Northern Select Foods Ltd

Michael J. Harrison   01748 811 555

Unit 12, Station Road Industrial Park, Brompton-on-Swale, Richmond, North Yorkshire DL10 7SN

F: 01748 811 777
E: info@ukselectfoods.co.uk
W: www.ukselectfoods.co.uk

Food wholesalers to hotels, restaurants, cafes, outside caterers, delicatessens and other retailers. Products range from fresh, chilled, frozen, through to roasted and dried goods. Delivering in the north east, Monday-Friday.

We stock a wide range of cheeses, meat products, ice-cream, fruit purees, sauces, and fresh mushrooms, herbs and eggs. Our range of dried goods is extensive for example; herbs and spices, flour, sugar, nuts, tinned produce, pasta and various pastry casings, dried fruit/veg our other vegetables include roasted and frozen.

Delivering real Yorkshire Creamy cheese

deliciously Yorkshire

deliciouslyYorkshire

deliciouslyorkshire

South Yorkshire

Think of South Yorkshire and your pavlovian response is likely to be 'mining' and 'steel'. Yet it is a county of contrasts.

Evidence of the area's wealth, built during the time of industrial innovation, remains in the many impressive country houses and stately homes. Yet Sheffield, England's fourth largest city, is also its greenest.

Situated just six miles from the Peak District which offers some of England's most spectacular scenery, the 'city of steel' dominates South Yorkshire. A strong industrial heritage is celebrated at many of the areas attractions such as the Cutler's Hall and science adventure centre Magna, at Rotherham.

Sheffield has hosted markets for more than 700 years and has a bustling weekly market. South Yorkshire's food credentials are proven, with over seventy farmers' markets taking place across the region and buzzing with a plethora of award-winning local fare – proof, if it were needed, that shopping locally with speciality producers is a much more exciting prospect than tackling the supermarket run.

Nearby Doncaster boasts one of the oldest markets in England, as well as its famous racecourse, home to the classic St Ledger.

South Yorkshire

South Yorkshire Food Highlights

Barnsley
3

Doncaster
4　2

Rotherham

1　**Sheffield**

Useful contacts

www.deliciouslyyorkshire.co.uk
www.yorkshire.com
www.sheffieldcity.co.uk
www.visitpeakdistrict.com
www.lincsuk.com
www.doncaster.gov.uk
www.syfarmersmarkets.co.uk

1 Coppice House Farm Shop Rivelin
Farm shop *(see entry on p116)*

2 McCallums Bank End Farm Shop
Farm shop *(see entry on p117)*

3 Round Green Farm Venison Company
Venison producer and shop *(see entry on p110)*

4 Wilkinson Butchers
Traditional butcher *(see entry on p116)*

deliciously**yorkshire**

deliciously yorkshire

Shops local – Sheffield

Sheffield is very much an up and coming Yorkshire city and is fast developing a lively food and drink scene.

England's fourth largest city has a long market tradition. Today is no exception, with a bustling wholesale flower and fresh produce market on Parkway Drive, Castle indoor market and a farmers' market still being held in the Castlegate area every week.

England's greenest city, Sheffield's close proximity to the Peak District enables it to offer a diverse mix of food producers and local products.

Here is a selection of just some of the best of the producers in this area.

For a full listing of all food and drink producers in this area see pages 108 to 117 or visit **www.deliciouslyyorkshire.co.uk** for contact details.

South Yorkshire

In and Around Town

Pollard's Tea and Coffee

Trading for over 130 years, Pollard's produces a range of quality tea and coffee, including making two coffees for the Brian Turner brand. This family-run coffee and tea business also has shops in Meadowhall and on Charles Street.

The Yorkshire Crisp Company

The Yorkshire Crisp Company was launched by Tony Bishop, a former farm manager and his business partner, Ashley Turner. They produce premium crisps made from the finest potatoes, hand cooked in batches and packaged in smart mini drums. Available from Sheffield Farmers' Market and selected outlets in the city and beyond.

Cunningham's

The firm has been producing high quality pickles and sauces for over 120 years and has enjoyed regional success with its piccalilli, strong and spicy pickled onions and a new product – Tigerlilli, which combines the well loved flavour of piccalilli with chillis and peppers. The range is available in Sainsbury's.

Round Green Farm Venison

Venison is one of the healthiest red meats as it's full of omega 6 and 3. So when owner Richard Elmhirst serves up his Round Green venison burgers at Sheffield Farmers' Market, shoppers always come flocking.

Dore Delicatessen

Located in Dore on the outskirts of Sheffield, this village deli features an extensive selection of cheeses as well as an olive bar. You can also order exclusive fine food hampers.

South **Yorkshire**

deliciouslyyorkshire

Shops local – Doncaster

Doncaster has one of the most vibrant markets in the North of England. After all, where else would you find 15 fishmongers, over 20 butchers, cheesemongers, bakers, delicatessens and cafés next to Chinese, Polish and even Caribbean grocers?

And that is only in the food halls. Almost every imaginable product is available somewhere on the market – the fun is finding it by exploring the whole place.

Doncaster Farmer's Market prides itself in offering the very best of local, national and international goods of the very highest quality, in a lively town centre location. So you can buy the freshest of local fayre whilst doing your city centre shopping in the same trip.

The area around Doncaster is also home to some of the region's best kept foodie secrets and Deliciouslyorkshire, the brand for fantastic food and drink from Yorkshire and Humber, aims to encourage people to shop locally and enjoy the great food on their doorstep.

Local Food

McCallums Bank End Farm Shop

Bank End Farm Shop is a showcase for excellent home grown produce available locally. Open throughout the year, the shop stocks a diverse range of products, from fresh fruit and vegetables to meat and fish that have been produced at Bank End Farm or by nearby farmers. Sample some of the goods on offer in the shop at McCallums café.

Cooplands

A chain of traditional Yorkshire bakeries, Cooplands offers an excellent selection of freshly prepared sandwiches and the freshest of bacon butties in a morning and at lunchtime. Cooplands, Queensgate, Baxter Lane and North Mall, Doncaster.

The Punjabi Curry Sauce Company

Raj Rani Singh creates traditional hand made curry sauces using family recipes. Perfect for pepping up locally sourced meat and vegetables. Look out for Punjabi Curry Sauces at South Yorkshire Farmer's Markets.

The Topping Pie Company

Topping Pies is a family run business specialising in high quality pies for prestige customers. The business, originally a retail butchers, began specialising in pie making in 1991. Since then it has scooped over 30 'Gold' Taste awards, both at home and internationally. All of Topping's Pies are made to original recipes by Maggie Topping and, thanks to their unsurpassed quality, even grace the director's hampers at Harrods.

Wilkinson's Butchers

Wilkinson's is a traditional family butcher, established in 1954 by Bernard Wilkinson and now run by Trevor and his son Daniel. The firm sells locally reared beef, pork and lamb and specialises in a large selection of award winning sausages. The team at Wilkinson's also cures their own hams and bacon.

Hotels and Eateries

Mount Pleasant Hotel

Since 1938, generations of visitors to Doncaster have enjoyed the unique country style and character of Mount Pleasant. Situated in 100 acres of wooded parkland between the market towns of Doncaster and Bawtry, this is an award winning AA Rosette Restaurant, serving excellent locally produced food.

The Crown at Bawtry

Having just undergone a £2.5million refurbishment, this well known gastro pub and hotel offers an excellent locally sourced menu as well as a comfortable place to rest your head. Chef and farmer's daughter Caroline Rhodes creates a menu ranging from local rack of lamb with rosemary and redcurrant sauce to locally reared venison terrine with Cumberland sauce.

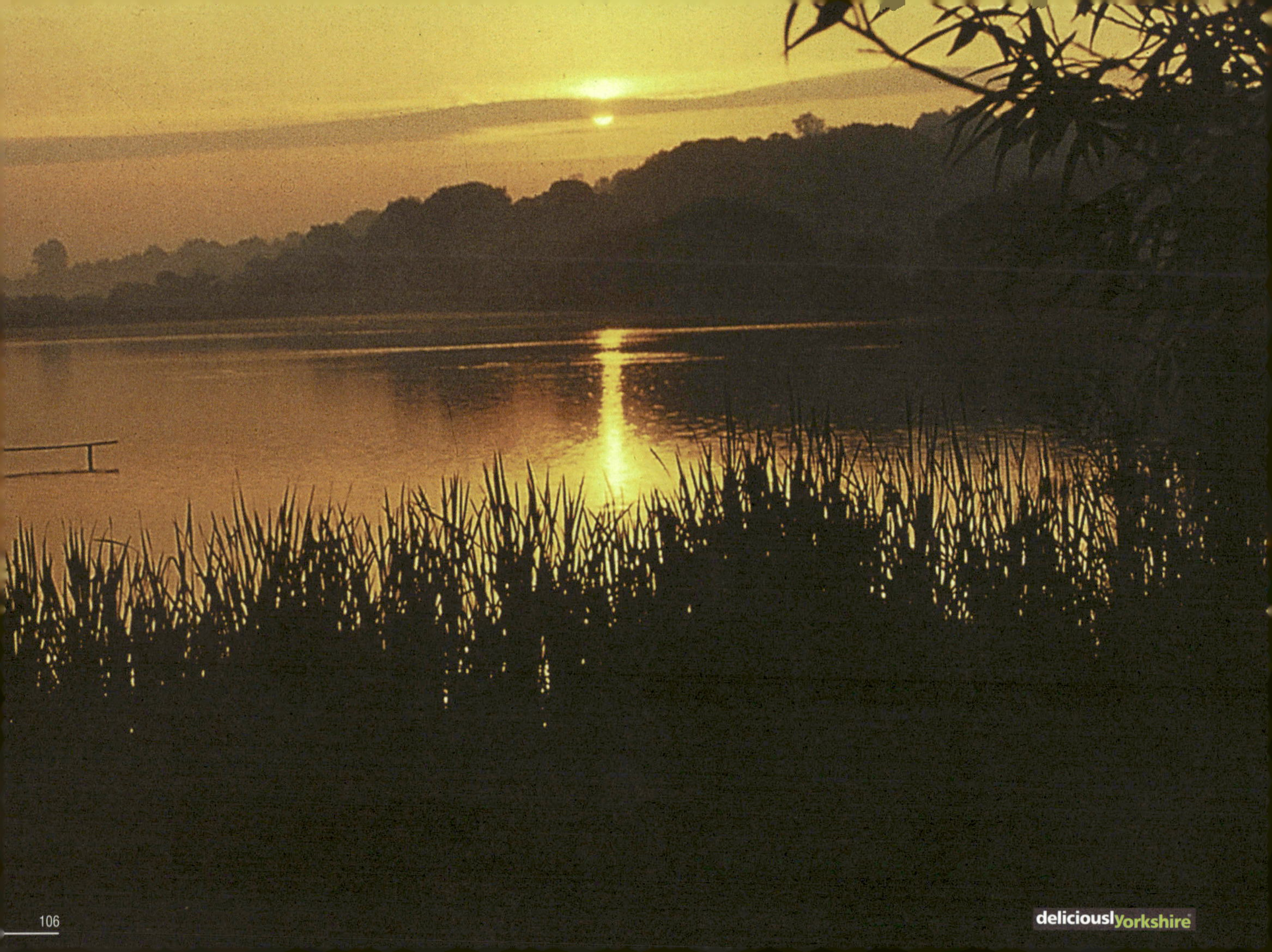

South Yorkshire Members

Producers

Bakers and confectioners

A L Simpkin & Co Ltd

Adrian Simpkin/Caroline Roney 01142 348 736

Hunter Road, Sheffield
South Yorkshire S6 4LD

F: 01142 325 635
E: enquiries@alsimpkin.com
W: www.alsimpkin.com / www.traditionalsweets.com

Since 1921 the Simpkin family have been manufacturing Glucose Travel Sweets. Made by traditional methods and recipes, incorporating only the finest ingredients and flavours available.

The "original English" travel tin range since 1921.
Sugar free/gluten free confectionery. Private label/contract manufacturers. UK and International Markets.

Cooplands

Robert McIlroy 01302 818 000

Victoria Mill Business Park, Wharf Road, Wheatley, Doncaster, South Yorkshire DN1 2SX

F: 01302 329 776
E: customer.service@cooplands.co.uk
W: www.cooplands.co.uk

Cooplands is Yorkshire's leading retail family bakers with over 70 shops throughout the region. Visit our website to order your personalised, handmade celebration cakes for collection from our nearest shop. Other party fayre including sandwich platters, quiches and gateaux will also soon be available. Save 10% when ordering online.

Delicious Alchemy

Emma Killilea 01142 655 033

12 Framlingham Road, Sheffield,
South Yorkshire S2 2GU

F: 01142 655 033
E: ekillilea@deliciousalchemy.co.uk
W: www.deliciousalchemy.co.uk

Delicious Alchemy supplies the highest quality wheat/gluten and lactose free food to hotels, restaurants and cafes.

The range includes bread loaves, rolls, pizza bases, burger buns, cakes and muesli.

Fosters Bakery Ltd

Bill Finnerty 01226 382 877

Towngate, Mapplewell,
Barnsley, South Yorkshire S75 6AS

F: 01226 390 087
E: bill@fostersbakery.co.uk
W: www.bake-it.com

Based in South Yorkshire, we are ideally placed to serve local and national retailers and caterers with premium quality bread, morning goods and confectionery.

South Yorkshire

Producers

Bakers and confectioners

Potts Bakers Ltd

Roger or Andrew Potts   01226 249 175

POTTS BAKERS

Stanley Road, Stairfoot, Barnsley,
South Yorkshire S70 3PG
- F: 01226 249 175
- E: potts.bakers@care4free.net
- W: www.pottsbakers.co.uk

Potts Bakers is a fourth generation business in Barnsley with five shops and a café in the Barnsley area. We supply wholesale to local retailers and sandwich shops, to the regional food service and to national retail markets. The 'Yorkshire's Finest' range of cakes will tempt visitors to garden centre and visitor attraction shops. We use high quality ingredients, locally sourced where possible. Our bread, savouries and cakes are made by skilled bakers, so the taste is just what you would expect from good home baking!

Sweets on the Menu

Lee Vintin/Wendy O'Brien   01142 835 948

Unit C 17 Alison Business Centre, 39 Alison Crescent, Sheffield, South Yorkshire S2 1AS
- E: wendy@sweetsonthemenu.co.uk
- W: www.sweetsonthemenu.co.uk

Sweets on the Menu can provide your restaurant, deli or café with high quality desserts, pastries and chocolates. We use locally sourced high quality produce where possible. Bespoke service also available.

The Real Bread Bakehouse Ltd

Emma Boardwell   01142 499 103 / 0780 9893781

5 Banner Cross Road, Sheffield,
South Yorkshire S11 9HQ
- E: getintouch@realbreadbakehouse.com
- W: www.realbreadbakehouse.comk

Artisan, organic bakery in Sheffield. Hand moulded bread and confectionery traditionally baked.

No additives or 'enhancers', just longer fermentation times to develop natural flavour, Bread as it should be.

Dairy and eggs

Amos Kaye

William Kaye   01226 763 134

Amos Kaye & Son

Townhead Farm, Dunford Bridge,
Sheffield, South Yorkshire S36 4TG

Amos Kaye & Son is a family business producing quality eggs from our own farm. Delivering to many areas.

Suppliers to all types of businesses including restaurants, cafes, public houses, nursing homes etc. Competitive prices and quality guaranteed.

South Yorkshire

Producers

South Yorkshire

00 see food highlight map on page 102

Beverages – alcoholic and non alcoholic

Pollards Tea & Coffee

Simon Bower 01142 617 517

Unit 15 E/F Tinsley Ind. Estate, Shepcote Lane,
Sheffield, South Yorkshire S9 1TL

F: 01142 445 309
E: hello@pollards.com
W: www.pollards.com

Producers of a range of quality tea & coffee, including two coffees for the Brian Turner brand. A family business which also has tea & coffee shops.

The Essential Food & Drink Company Limited

Peter Moulam 01142 755 971

25 Cardwell Drive, Sheffield,
South Yorkshire S13 7XD

E: p.moulam@talktalk.net
W: www.citrus-hits.co.uk

Citrus Hits are a refreshing and natural drink combining infusions of herbs and fruits with fresh citrus juice. Featuring local ingredients, low sugar and no preservatives, Citrus Hits are a fantastic taste experience.

Wentworth Brewery Ltd

Steven Beech 01226 747 070

The Powerhouse, Gun Park, Wentworth,
South Yorkshire S62 7TF

F: 01226 747 050
E: info@wentworth-brewery.co.uk
W: www.wentworth-brewery.co.uk

Brewery suppliers of cask and bottled beers. Bottled spring water. All Yorkshire region supplied.

Fact! The region produces almost a third of the UK's beer

Meat, poultry and game – fresh and smoked

3 Round Green Farm Venison Company

Richard Elmhirst 08456 120 502

Round Green Farm, Worsbrough,
Barnsley, South Yorkshire S75 3DR

F: 01226 281 294
E: info@roundgreenfarm.co.uk
W: www.roundgreenfarm.co.uk

Venison from Round Green Farm is available in many forms e.g. steak, joints, sausage, casserole, liver, pies, pate, smoked.

Less fat than chicken, good omega 3, high iron, means healthy red meat. Being from young farmed stock it is succulent, tender, and very easy to cook. Phone to learn more!

deliciouslyyorkshire

Producers

Meat, poultry and game – fresh and smoked

Sutcliffe Farmers Ltd

Andrew Sutcliffe   01302 772 216

Highwood Farm, Misson,
Doncaster, South Yorkshire DN10 6PP

E: sutcliffefarmersltd@eurotelbroadband.com

Milk and meat producers. We retail to farm shops and farmers markets. We sell all local produce.

Pies

The Topping Pie Company

Roger Topping   01302 738 333

Unit 2 Chappell Drive, Waterside Industrial Estate, Doncaster, South Yorkshire DN1 2RF

F: 01302 738 366
E: mail@toppingspies.co.uk

The Topping Pie Company are manufacturers of speciality Gold Award winning pork pies and quiches.

A total of 21 gold awards have been received by Toppings during the last 8 years, besides awards for the best Speciality Producer of the Year 2003, Best in Yorkshire 2002 and 2001 and an award for innovation in 2001.

Prepared food

Cornscape

Steve Seddon   01226 709 332

Unit 14 Albion Road, Carlton Industrial Estate, Barnsley, South Yorkshire S71 3HW

F: 01226 728 535
E: info@cornscape.co.uk
W: www.cornscape.co.uk

Gourmet recipes of toffee popcorn with inclusions and organic popcorn packed in premium packaging.

Popcorn as inclusions for food processors in their recipes.

GW Price

Debre Willoughby   01246 432 818

13 High Street, Eckington,
South Yorkshire S21 4DH

E: nigel@gwprice.co.uk
W: www.gwprice.co.uk

Wholesale fruit and potato merchants and importers. Prepared fruit and vegetable specialists.

Producers

Prepared food

King Asia Foods Ltd

Dan Suh   01302 760 070

Middle Bank, Doncaster,
South Yorkshire DN4 5JJ

F: 01302 760 386
E: dansuh@kingasia.co.uk
W: www.kingasia.co.uk

King Asia Foods are the leading manufacturers of oriental food in the frozen food industry. Our 50,000 sq ft factory produces over 15 million meals a year. We pride ourselves on providing the highest quality oriental food solutions for foodservice and retail markets. For more information, please look at www.kingasia.co.uk or call us on 01302 760 070.

Punjabi Curry Sauce Company

Raj Rani Singh   01302 761 024

2B Sandall Stone, Kirk Sandall,
Doncaster, South Yorkshire DN2 1QR

F: 01302 761 024

Traditional hand made curry sauces produced using only traditional family recipes and authentic ingredients. Our sauces include Rogan, Korma, Passanda, Madras, Tikka, Mild, Vindaloo, Bhuna and Dopiaza.

The Real Yorkshire Pudding Company Ltd

Deirdre Bailey   01405 815 523

Coulman Road Industrial Estate, Thorne,
Doncaster, South Yorkshire DN8 5JS

F: 01405 817 710
E: dbailey@realyorks.co.uk
W: www.realyorks.co.uk

The Real Yorkshire Pudding Company have been making premium quality Yorkshire Puddings, chilled and frozen for over 12 years.

Our puddings are made to a traditional recipe using only fresh ingredients. For more information contact us on 01405 815 523.

Producers

Prepared food

Yorkshire Crisp Company

Tracey Fish   01909 774 411

Unit 2A Waleswood Industrial Estate,
Wales Bar, South Yorkshire S26 5PY

F: 01909 773 366
E: headfryer@yorkshirecrisps.co.uk
W: www.yorkshirecrisps.co.uk

Yorkshire Crisps: Your local hand-made crisp producer. Made with local produce and completely natural flavourings, not a preservative or trace of MSG in sight! Presented in unique and attractive packaging and available in 100g barrels, 50g bags and 500g catering packs in eight mouth watering flavours.

Preserves, honey, condiments and spices

Catherines Choice

David Trickett   07836 345 858

59 Westbourne Road, Broomhill,
Sheffield, South Yorkshire S10 2QT

F: 08707 058 856
E: sales@catherineschoice.plus.com

Producers of bespoke Great Taste Award winning preserves/fruit curds.

All of our products are additive and gluten free. Ingredients are sourced as locally as possible.

Glenroyd House Preserves

Michelle Roper-Shaw   07908 140 611

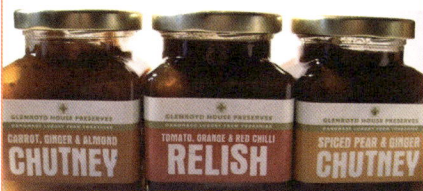

208 Dodworth Road, Barnsley,
South Yorkshire S70 6PF

F: 01226 730 809
E: info@glenroydhousepreserves.co.uk
W: www.glenroydhousepreserves.co.uk

We produce luxury preserves, bottled fruits in liqueur, fruit liqueurs and gift hampers.

All of our products are handmade in small batches in our own kitchen using organic fruit and vegetables.

We use seasonal ingredients and our product range changes throughout the year to complement the seasons.

South Yorkshire

Producers

Preserves, honey, condiments and spices

Cunningham Foods Ltd

Simon Webster   01142 577 899

239 High Street, Sheffield,
South Yorkshire S35 9XB

F: 01629 640 039
E: simonw@novantia.co.uk
W: www.novantia.co.uk

Cunninghams have been producing high quality pickles and sauces for over 120 years. A loyal brand following in South Yorkshire has now grown and Cunninghams is now available nationally throughout Sainsbury's.

Sheff's Special

John and Cath Tilney   01142 356 362

372 Ecclesall Road South,
Sheffield, South Yorkshire S11 9PY

E: chef@sheffs-special.co.uk
W: www.sheffs-special.co.uk

Sheff's Special is a family business. Our main product is MOJO, a green chilli sauce made with fresh lime and coriander. All our food is free from artificial additives.

Hospitality

Hotels and restaurants

Crown Hotel

Caroline Rhodes   01302 710 341

the crown hotel bawtry

High Street, Bawtry, Doncaster,
South Yorkshire DN10 6JW

F: 01302 711 798
E: events@crownhotel-bawtry.com
W: www.crownhotel-bawtry.com

The Crown Hotel has recently completed its £3 million refurbishment. Our new restaurant is the toast of the region. Our brand new menu which comprises locally sourced and produced food is prepared by our own award winning chef and her team. Whether on business or taking a short break, the 76 newly refurbished contemporary and stylish rooms, including 10 executive rooms, are another feature. Unlike other hotels, we have managed to combine all modern facilities with a charm and character that's now hard to find. Anywhere else is just a hotel!

Hellaby HALL Hotel

John Silker   08708 502 598

Old Hellaby Lane, Rotherham,
South Yorkshire S66 8SN

E: johnsilker@hellabyhallhotel.co.uk
W: www.hellabyhallhotel.co.uk

Steeped in history, Hellaby Hall Hotel's 17th Century building is an unmistakeable feature of the South Yorkshire skyline. The hotel proudly offers its guests a rarely found package of period charm and modern convenience.

Skilfully

deliciouslyyorkshire

Hospitality

Hotels and restaurants

Mount Pleasant Hotel

David Rowley 01302 868 696

Great North Road, Rossington,
Doncaster, South Yorkshire DN11 0HW

F: 01302 865 130
E: reception@mountpleasant.co.uk
W: www.mountpleasant.co.uk

Mount Pleasant Hotel is Doncaster's only four star hotel, set in 100 acres of wooded parkland and situated between Doncaster and Bawtry near Robin Hood Airport.

We provide the perfect setting for weddings, banquets, meetings and conferences.

Our AA Rosette restaurant offers the finest cuisine and extensive wine list.

Outside caterers

Food for Thought Ltd

Andy Gabbitas 01142 347 409

Woodside House, 355 Loxley Road,
Sheffield, South Yorkshire S6 4TH

F: 01142 347 409
E: info@foodforthought.uk.net
W: www.foodforthought.uk.net

Food for Thought, catering at it's finest! Dedicated to producing a unique, personal approach to food and entertaining in South Yorkshire.

Luxury

Retailers

Deli and independent grocers

Inspired Eating

Jon and Debbie Broadhurst 01142 353 569

E: sales@inspiredeating.co.uk
W: www.inspiredeating.co.uk

Inspired Eating specialise in bespoke Yorkshire food gifts for the corporate market and provide a comprehensive hamper service from our website, with a distinct Yorkshire flavour.

For more information or to discuss your particular requirements contact us on 01142 353 569 or look at our fabulous range of hampers on www.inspiredeating.co.uk

South Yorkshire

deliciouslyyorkshire

Retailers

00 see food highlight map on page 102

Deli and independent grocers

Dore Delicatessen

Catherine Trickett   01142 368 574

40 High Street, Sheffield,
South Yorkshire S17 3GU

F: 08707 058 856
E: deli@catherineschoice.plus.com

Delicatessen selling a wide range of ambient & chilled high quality foods. We buy as locally as possible and concentrate on lesser known brands, our chef produces delightful quiches, cheeses, biscuits & cakes.

Sweetly

4 Wilkinson Butchers Ltd

Trevor Wilkinson   01302 365 834

Wilkinson Butchers
Three Generations of Quality and Service.

25 Market Hall, Doncaster,
South Yorkshire DN1 1NG

E: enquiries@wilkinson-butchers.co.uk
W: www.wilkinson-butchers.co.uk

Wilkinson Butchers began trading in 1954. We are a traditional family butchers now in our third generation, selling locally farmed Yorkshire Beef, Pork and Lamb. We specialise in a large selection of sausages which have won multiple awards and also cure our own bacon. We have shops in Doncaster and Bawtry and have recently launched a website, where you can purchase online our award winning sausages, and dry cured bacon, with seasonal special offers.

Farm shops

1 Coppice House Farm Shop Rivelin

Mick Ducker   01142 308 155

Coppice House Farm, Rivelin Valley Road,
Sheffield, South Yorkshire S6 5SG

E: shop@coppicehousefarmshop.co.uk
W: www.coppicehousefarmshop.co.uk

We are a friendly family run business operating from the farm. We sell our own or locally reared beef, lamb, pork, chicken and a wide range of fresh fruit & vegetables.

We also supply a variety of luxury jams, honey, pickles, cheeses and dairy products. Also on site holiday cottages.

South Yorkshire

deliciouslyyorkshire

Retailers

Farm shops

2 McCallums Bank End Farm Shop

David McCallum 01302 770 224

McCallums FARM FRESH FOODS

Bank End Road, Finningley,
Doncaster, South Yorrkshire DN9 3NT

F: 01302 770 224
E: davidmccallum@bt.com
W: www.mccallumfarm.co.uk

McCallums is a family business committed to pleasing our customers, priding ourselves on quality, dedication and particularly fresh produce.

We have created a friendly pleasing environment for our customers whether visiting the farmshop/café or simply coming to pick your own fruit.

Do visit us online.

Distributors

Country Fresh Foods

Neil Dowker 01142 481 188

Unit 2c Meadow Brook Park, Halfway,
Sheffield, South Yorkshire S20 3PJ

E: neil@countryfreshfoods.co.uk
W: www.countryfreshfoods.co.uk

Yorkshire's premier chilled food distributor. Tell us what you want and we will deliver. Our commitment to delivering quality and service is second to none and true to our motto 'by caterers for caterers'.

Fruitily

00 see food highlight map on page 102

Fact!

Yorkshire and Humber has the largest concentration of food and drink in the UK and is a world-leading centre of excellence

South Yorkshire

deliciously yorkshire

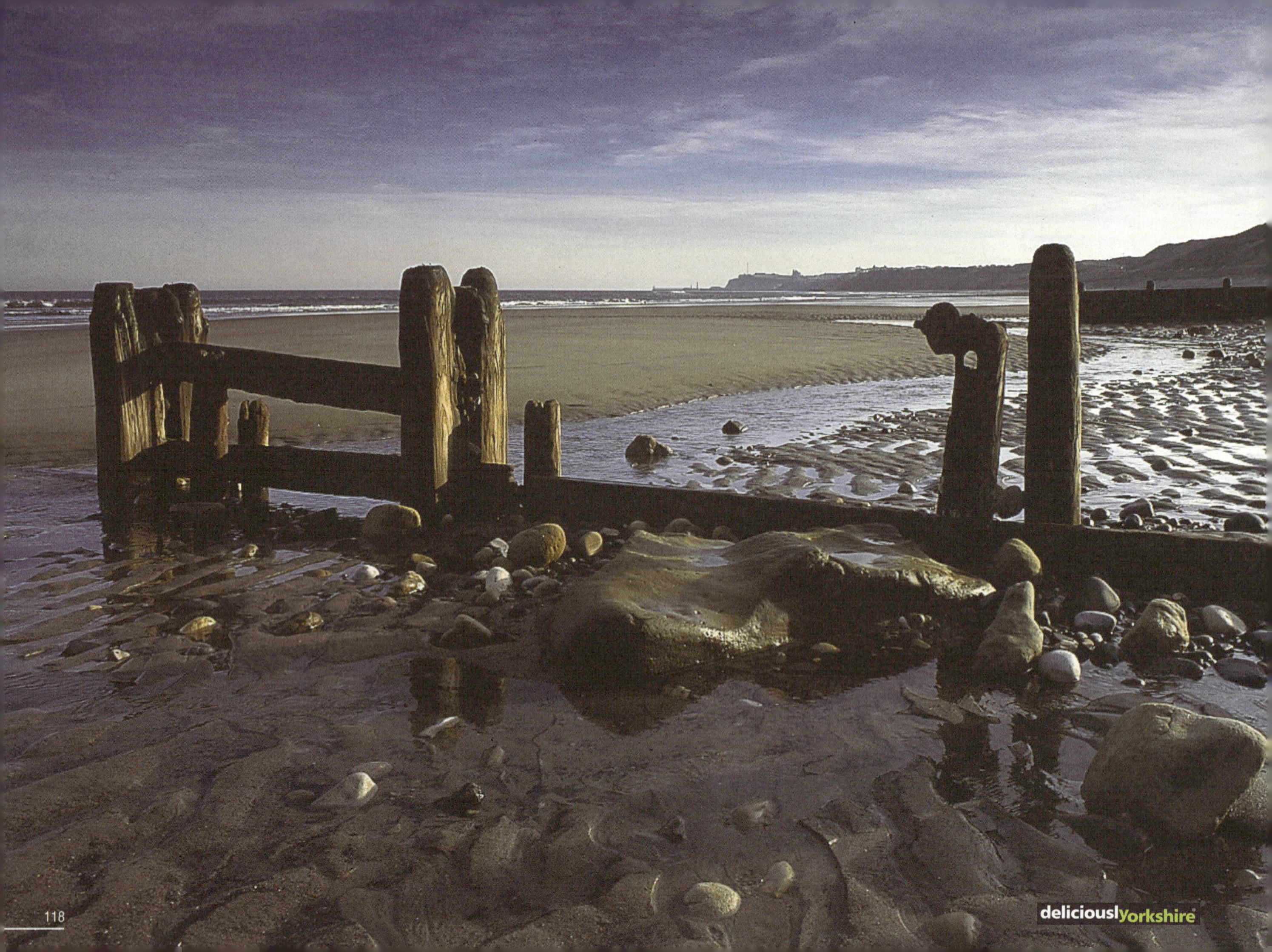

East Yorkshire

East Yorkshire seems a world away – and one of contrasts. From the golden sands of its traditional family-friendly resorts to the dramatic cliffs and lighthouse of Flamborough Head and the nature-rich Spurn Point which divides the North Sea from the Humber.

Award-winning sandy beaches for endless fun with the family. Picturesque villages for a perfect pub lunch. Gently undulating countryside for walking including the 79-mile Wolds Way National Trail, cycling, even horseriding. Unspoilt havens for birds, butterflies, wildflowers and marine life. Medieval minsters and historic houses for culture vultures.

The city of Hull offers a stunning waterfront location and stands at the gateway to the Humber bridge – the world's third largest suspension bridge – while East Yorkshire's historic market towns have a unique character of their own. Beverley's narrow, medieval streets are full of antique shops and craft arcades and there are regular music festivals. Driffield, affectionately known as Capital of the Wolds, holds one of the county's largest agricultural shows every year.

Stately homes abound. Burton Constable Hall, Sewerby Hall and Gardens, Burton Agnes Hall and Sledmere House are filled with priceless treasures and surrounded by magnificent gardens, none finer than Burnby Hall Gardens, with Europe's largest water lily collection. Outdoor activities are also well catered for with sailing, rowing, fishing, bowling, shooting, golf, even jet-skiing and gliding – the choice is endless.

East Yorkshire

East Yorkshire Food Highlights

Map locations:
- Bridlington
- Driffield
- Market Weighton
- Beverley
- Hull

1 Burton Agnes Hall Farmer's Food Store
Farm shop (see entry on p135)

2 Costello's
Craft bakery (see entry on p134)

3 Kelleythorpe Farm Shop
Farm shop (see entry on p135)

4 Manor Farm Shop
Farm shop (see entry on p136)

5 Mr Moo's Real Dairy Ice Cream
Ice cream (see entry on p128)

6 The Pipe & Glass Inn
Country inn (see entry on p134)

Useful contacts

www.deliciouslyyorkshire.co.uk
www.eastriding.gov.uk
www.visiteastyorkshire.co.uk
www.hull.co.uk
www.yorkshire.com

deliciouslyyorkshire

deliciouslyorkshire

Shops local – Beverley

East Yorkshire has more than its fair share of pretty market towns, selling fresh, high quality produce. Here is a selection of just some of them. For a full listing of all food and drink producers in this area see pages 126 to 136 or visit www.deliciouslyorkshire.co.uk for contact details. Here's a pick of some of the best.

Beverley, a pretty market town with a racing heritage, is nestled in the beautiful scenery of the Yorkshire Wolds, where if you travel in from the West, you get a fantastic view of the town's Minster, as well as the ever-green Beverley Westwood. Along there, you may even encounter cattle grazing precariously close to the road, which all sets up an appealing and unique entrance to the town.

If you descend into Beverley on a Saturday you'll experience an old fashioned market as it should be. Bustling flower, fruit and veg stalls combine to create the appropriately named Saturday Market, which takes place in the town's cobbled market square alongside the Historic Market Cross.

East Yorkshire

Places to Stay
Tickton Grange

This is a country house hotel set in beautiful grounds just on the outskirts of the town. With two AA rosettes and a local food sourcing initiative, you can be eating Sancton goat's cheese, locally grown asparagus or Kellythorpe beef in Hambleton ale.

Local Food on Menus
The Pipe and Glass Inn

Chef and proprietor James Mackenzie has built up a truly enviable reputation at this recently renovated and specially situated gastro pub. Based in a real gem of an East Yorkshire village – South Dalton, the pub offers London quality food at reasonable prices. Choose from the likes of locally sourced rib of Skerne beef with Yorkshire pudding followed by ginger burnt cream with stewed Yorkshire rhubarb.

deliciouslyorkshire annual awards Winner 2006

Sweetly Local
Just Puds

Based in Woodmansey near Beverley, this luxury puddings firm has scooped awards for its sticky toffee and saucy chocolate puddings, as well as its indulgent butterscotch sauce.

Drink Local
The White Horse

A food and drink article about Beverley wouldn't be complete without an obligatory mention to local boozer The White Horse, or Nellies as it's known by locals. This ancient inn has been trading for over 350 years (at least – records show it may be even longer), and still boasts original features.

East Yorkshire

deliciouslyorkshire®

Shops local – Driffield

Driffield, or 'the capital of the Wolds' as it is lovingly known by locals, is a real find. If only to witness how a close community of people can support local shopping both in town and at the thriving farmers' market at its showground.

Choose from local suppliers of bacon, pies and healthy snacks at the farmers' market, to baked goods and skilled butchers in town. Driffield also has a buzzing social scene, thanks to its well run pubs, bars and clubs and a local clientele who are always up for a good time.

Take a look in the alphabetical index or visit www.deliciouslyorkshire.co.uk for full contact details of the following pick of the best.

In and Around Town

Wold Top Brewery
Farming family the Mellors' Wold Top Brewery benefits from its own borehole supplying the purest chalk filtered water for its beers. If you're arranging an event they can even bring you a Wold Top Bar from which to serve your beer.

The Side Oven Bakery
This family run firm creates traditionally baked fresh breads and croissants using the farm's original side oven. The company only uses locally grown stoneground wheat, which preserves the vital nutrients in flour, so often lost with today's milling process.

Shepcote of Driffield
Creating the finest of hand made cake decorations and marzipan confectionery.

East Yorkshire

Rose Cottage Foods
Making traditional fruit and pork pies from the best local ingredients, this Driffield based company is going from strength to strength.

Blue Keld Springs
Blue Keld is a mineral water straight from the chalky springs of the Wolds, and is so popular with the locals that it's now also available for Londoners on the Hull Train services to King's Cross.

Burton Agnes Hall Farmer's Food Store
Visit this stunning Elizabethan hall and its popular farm shop for a taste of local produce in an environment which leaves you feeling you've just stepped off the set of a BBC costume drama.

Mr Moo's Real Dairy Ice Cream
Lovingly billed as 'beautiful ice cream' by celebrity chef Brian Turner, this family run business is attracting an increasing number of visitors to its base in Skipsea near Driffield. Mr Moo's wonderfully high quality ice cream is churned fresh from the farm's own herd of Friesians and comes in flavours from locally produced lavender and honey to seasonal fruits.

Farmers' Markets
Driffield Farmers' Market is held at the town's showground on the first Saturday of every month from 9am - 1pm.

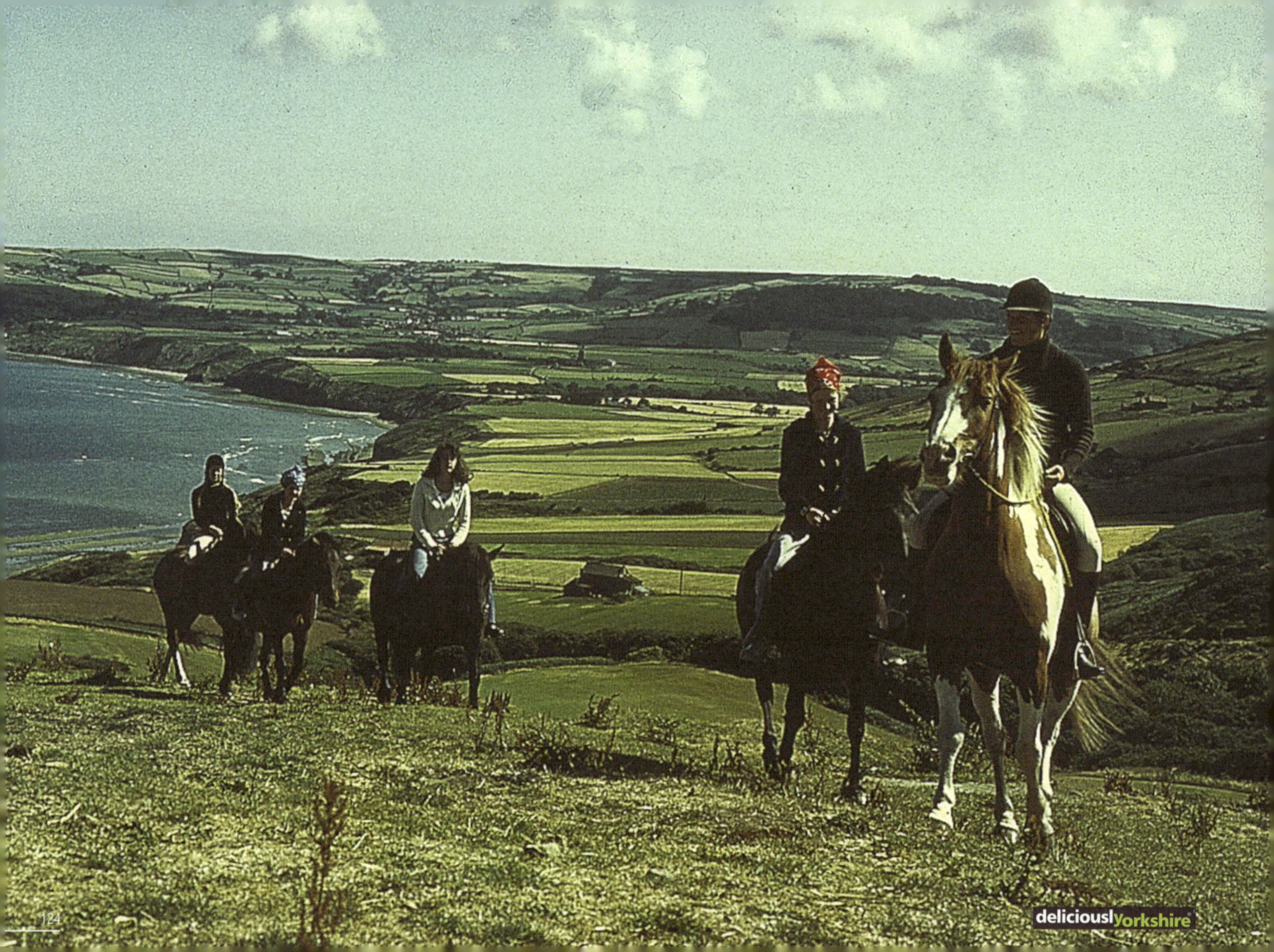

East Yorkshire Members

Producers

Bakers and confectioners

Just Puds Limited

Annabelle Hughes   0870 112 9545

Petunia House, Plaxton Bridge Road, Woodmansey,
Beverley, East Yorkshire HU17 0RT

- F: 0870 112 9544
- E: enquiries@justpuds.co.uk
- W: www.justpuds.co.uk

Since 1999, Rosemary Robinson has been bringing the joys of family baking to the masses. Starting from the farmhouse kitchen, she stocked local farmers markets and delicatessens, demand soon outstripped supply, and a larger BRC accredited bakery found.

Now in it's 8th year, Just Puds has continued to grow in success and achieved a number of prestigious awards. Simplicity and integrity combined with sheer indulgence.

Kitchen

Debbie Masters   07775 772 496

Atlantica, Lowgate, Balne,
Nr Goole, East Yorkshire DN14 0ED

- F: 01405 861 913

At Kitchen we produce beautiful breads, pretty pastries & supa-dupa meringues.

All handmade with extra care & attention in our farm yard bakery.

Pattacakes

Anita Tasker   01759 377 392

Catton House Farm, 18 Main Street, Stamford Bridge,
York, East Yorkshire YO41 1AB

- F: 01759 377 392
- E: tasker@stamford.a-i-s.co.uk
- W: www.pattacakes.co.uk

Small patisserie & outside catering business producing a range of elegant cakes, pastries, gateaux, wedding cakes and puddings. My produce is of the highest quality and that little bit different.

Side Oven Bakery

Caroline Sellers   01262 488 376

Carr House Farm, Foston-on-the-Wolds,
Driffield, East Yorkshire YO25 8BS

- F: 01262 488 376
- E: bakery@sideoven.com
- W: www.sideoven.com

Organic bakery producing traditionally baked breads & croissants using home grown organic wheat & wood burning oven.

Also available stoneground flour & honey toasted mueslis.

Producers

Bakers and confectioners

The Ultimate Candy Company Limited

David Richardson 01482 891 754

4 Sheriff Highway, Hedon,
East Yorkshire HU12 8HD
- F: 01482 897 378
- E: ultimatecandy@aol.com

Ultimate Candy's award winning, hand broken, 16% butter fudge is but one of many products available within their range. Chocolate lovers adore our chocolate crumble mints - soft, mint centres, coated in thick plain chocolate. For indulgence, fairtrade, organic and sugar free contact us now.

Dairy and eggs

J A Carlile Farms Ltd

Carolyn Batty 01430 871 177 ext 25

Mile House Farm, Holme Road,
Market Weighton, East Yorkshire YO43 3EU
- F: 01430 871 188
- E: jacarlilefarms@btopenworld.com

Fresh lion quality eggs, produced and packed on farm with free delivery into Yorkshire and Lincolnshire.

Crumbly

Lowna Dairy Ltd

Tom and Tricia Wallis 01482 670 570 / 656 588

Raywell, Cottingham,
East Yorkshire HU16 5YL
- F: 01482 656 779
- E: dairy@lownadairy.com
- W: www.lownadairy.com

The gently rolling hills of East Yorkshire are home to the Lowna herd of milk producing goats.

Tom and Tricia hand make their cheeses in small batches at the Lowna Dairy and each cheese is fresh and distinctly finished with flavours varying with the changing seasons. Introducing GoPukka Ltd as our new delivery arm.

East Yorkshire

deliciouslyorkshire

Producers

00 see food highlight map on page 120

Dairy and eggs

5 Mr Moo's Real Dairy Ice Cream

Stephen Foreman   01262 469 829

Southfield House Farm, Skipsea,
Driffield, East Yorkshire YO25 8SY

F: 01262 468 209
E: info@mrmoos.co.uk
W: www.mrmoos.co.uk

Mr Moo's Dairy Ice Cream ia a product that brings back memories of ice cream as it used to be. Its simple, rich, creamy flavour using milk from the family farm & where possible, locally sourced ingredients makes this an ice cream that will delight even the most discerning customer.

Beverages – alcoholic and non alcoholic

Blue Keld Springs Ltd

Belle Marr   01377 271 207

Throstle Nest, Cranswick,
Driffield, East Yorkshire YO25 9RE

F: 01377 271 360
E: info@bluekeld.co.uk
W: www.bluekeld.co.uk

Blue Keld Spring Ltd natural mineral water is sourced from an ancient artesian spring situated on the edge of the Yorkshire Wolds. The crystal clear waters are filtered through chalk over many years eventually bubbling up to the surface at the artesian 'Keld'. We produce a wide range of products from sugar free natural fruit flavoured water in plastic bottles to natural mineral water in our unique blue glass tear drop shaped bottle. Now available Blue Keld Premium spring water ice cubes produced from a brand new state of the art factory capable of producing 20,000 bags per day.

Wold Top Brewery

Tom/Gill Mellor   01723 892 222

Hunmanby Grange, Wold Newton,
Driffield, East Yorkshire YO25 3HS

F: 01723 892 229
E: enquiries@woldtopbrewery.co.uk
W: www.woldtopbrewery.co.uk

The Wold Top Brewery on a Yorkshire Wold farm, brews by tradtional methods, utilising its own chalk filtered water and wold grown barley, to produce a range of beers, each with a uniqueness of character and strength to provide for all occasions, in casks or bottles ... grown on the wolds, brewed on the wolds, drunk anywhere ...

Producers

Fish – fresh and smoked

Simpson's

David Orr 01482 585 109

35 West Dock Street,
Hull, East Yorkshire HU3 4HH

E: david@simpson-seafish.co.uk
W: www.simpson-seafish.co.uk

One of the largest independent family owned companies in the UK producing a range of chilled, smoked and frozen products for the UK and overseas markets.

Fresh ingredients

Foxton Country Fresh

Paul Foxton 01482 811 440

The Beeches, Manor Farm, Coniston,
Hull, East Yorkshire HU11 4JX

F: 01482 815 245
E: foxton.farmers.ltd@farmline.com
W: www.foxtoncountryfresh.com

Providers of potato specialities. From par-cooked chunky chips to whole baby roasts, our range of fresh Yorkshire produce combines great taste with reduced cooking times for your catering convenience.

Ingredient suppliers

Aarhus Karlshamn

Rachel Neale 01482 701 271

King George Dock,
Hull, East Yorkshire HU9 5PX

F: 01482 709 447
E: rachel.neale@aak.com
W: www.aarhuskarlshamn.com

Aarhus Karlshamn (AAK) is a leading supplier of speciality fats and oils. The company has the broadest product range in the industry and is second to none in the ability to offer cost efficient, added value solutions to customers in the food, confectionery and cosmetics industries.

Humdinger Ltd

Phil Whitfield 01482 625 790

Gothenburg Way, Sutton Fields Ind Estate,
Hull, East Yorkshire HU7 0YG

F: 01482 625 791
E: sales@humdinger-foods.co.uk
W: www.humdinger-foods.co.uk

Humdinger Ltd is a leading supplier of grocery products within the UK and in partnership with one of our principals, Sunsweet Growers Inc, we also have an extensive European presence.

Producers

Ingredient suppliers

Shepcote Distributors

E R Shepherdson   01377 252 537

Pexton Road, Kelleythorpe Industrial Estate,
Driffield, East Yorkshire YO25 9DJ

F: 01377 252 539
E: enquiries@shepcote.com
W: www.shepcote.com

Shepcote was established in 1969 and has built an enviable reputation as manufacturers of top quality hand made cake decorations and almond marzipan confectionery. Made to a traditional recipe and skilfully hand finished our fruits are appreciated by consumers not only across the UK but on occasions even further afield. Testament to the consistent quality, flavour and appearance we regularly supply bluechip companies, major tourist attractions and nationally known London stores. We also carry an extensive range of dried fruits, nuts, seeds and gift confectionery.

Meat, poultry and game – fresh and smoked

Beef Improvement Grouping Ltd

Richard Fuller   07970 097 519

Southburn Office, Driffield,
East Yorkshire YO25 9ED

F: 01759 368 174
E: richard.fuller@jsr.co.uk

Lush green pastures high on the Yorkshire Wolds where careful Stewardship of the countryside encourages abundant wildlife. This is Givendale Prime country home of free-range beef that's the best of British. Available at family butcher Bill Burton in Pocklington at the foot of the Yorkshire Wolds.

East Riding Country Pork

Mrs R Buckle   01964 671 137

Dalton Lane, Halsham,
Hull, East Yorkshire HU12 0DG

F: 01964 671 137
E: info@eastridingcountrypork.co.uk
W: www.eastridingcountrypork.co.uk

At East Riding Country Pork we take great pride in producing the very best prime quality pork meat and maintain our high standards by controlling the whole pig rearing process.

Speciality

deliciouslyyorkshire

Producers

Meat, poultry and game – fresh and smoked

J H & M Burton

Grant Burton   01759 380 244

Manor House Farm, Wilberfoss,
York, East Yorkshire YO41 5NY

E: grant@wilberfoss.com

Burtons of Wilberfoss produce the highest quality pork, sausages and dry cured bacon from our own herd of free range pigs. Our sausages, bacon and all other meat products are made from our home-reared pork ensuring full traceability. The highest quality herbs and spices are used. Careful attention is paid to ensuring that all our 24 varieties of sausage have a low fat content and are made from the highest quality meat. We attend a large number of farmers markets and also supply hotels, restaurants and shops. Product is delivered in our refrigerated transport.

Lamb-In-A-Box

John or Sally   01377 270 788

J.H. Medforth, Rotsea Manor, Rotsea,
Cranswick, Driffield, East Yorkshire YO25 9QG

E: sales@lamb-in-a-box.co.uk
W: www.lamb-in-a-box.co.uk

Traditionally reared Lamb and Mutton, jointed, labelled and delivered fresh to your door, in half or full boxes.

The Lambs are farmed as they were in our Grandparents era, on their mothers milk, grazing mainly on unfertilised Yorkshire Wolds land, with as little intervention from us as possible. They are as-near-as-damn-it-Organic.

Pies

Rose Cottage Foods Ltd

Rupert Clemmit   01377 257 700

Unit 17 Kelleythorpe Industrial Estate,
Driffield, East Yorkshire YO25 9DJ

E: rosecottagefoods@aol.com

Rose Cottage Foods produce award winning pies. They are made using only the finest quality ingredients.

Our products can be found at farmers markets and events throughout Yorkshire.

Naturally

Producers

Prepared food

Chaucer Foods Ltd

Richard Brewer 01482 588 088

Freightliner Road, Hull,
East Yorkshire HU3 4UN
F: 01482 588 082
E: sales@chaucerfoods.com
W: www.chaucerfoods.com

Chaucer Foods is a global supplier of croutons, toppings, sprinkles and snacks, as well as freeze dried ingredients to industrial, food service and retail customers.

Fruitface Fresh Nutrition

Edward Sweeting 01430 440 406

Thornton Lands, Foxfleet, Howden,
Goole, East Yorkshire DN14 7YR
E: healthy@fruitface.co.uk
W: www.fruitface.co.uk

Fruitface is a farm based business that supplies healthy and delicious snacks and ingredients made from fruits and seeds. We use our home grown linseed and mix it with other seeds and dried fruits. Deliciously healthy! We supply a range of outlets including delis, farm shops, and also sell online at www.fruitface.co.uk

Funky Snack Company

Richard Brewer 01482 588 088

Funky Land, Hull,
East Yorkshire HU4 4UN
F: 01482 588 082
E: sales@chaucerfoods.com
W: www.thefunkysnackcompany.co.uk

The Funky Snack Company is a manufacturer of innovative and deliciously different bread based snacks that are available in various retail outlets throughout the UK. Try them today!

William Jackson & Son Ltd

Richard Milner 01482 224 939

40 Darringham Street,
Hull, East Yorkshire HU3 1EW
E: richardmilner@wjs.co.uk
W: www.wjs.co.uk

William Jackson & Son is a fifth generation family business established in 1851 and based in Hull. Our manufacturing capabilities include chilled ready meal production, salad processing, fresh vegetable preparation and bakery. We are also the home of Aunt Bessie's range of Yorkshire puddings and traditional English Foods.

Producers

Prepared food

Yorkshire Hemp Limited

Paul Jenkinson   01924 375 475

PO Box 120, Driffield,
East Yorkshire YO25 9YS

F: 01924 374 068
E: info@yorkshirehemp.com
W: www.yorkshirehemp.com

Yorkshire Hemp Limited provide both certified organic and conventional bulk hemp seeds, shelled hemp seeds, roasted hemp seeds, hemp flour, hemp oil, hemp sauce and the essential oil of hemp to the baking, food manufacturing and nutraceutical industry.

Yorkshire Hemp's own brand of certified organic hemp and vegan hemp body care products are available through wholesale and retail outlets.

Preserves, honey, condiments and spices

Kitchen Guru

Chandra Parma   01132 669 390

Petunia Lakeside Park, Plaxton Bridge Road,
Woodmansey, Beverley, East Yorkshire HU17 0RT

E: info@kitchenguru.co.uk
W: www.kitchenguru.co.uk

Cook hassle-free real authentic Indian meals at home with the freshest taste. Winner of 10 prestigious awards, hassle free cooking, Truly Authentic, Freshest Taste, No Waste, Finest herbs & spices, No additives, preservatives or artificial colouring. Contact us for a free sample pack.

The best selling cook-at-home Indian meal kits.
Visit our brand new website for more information at www.kitchenguru.co.uk

Rebori

Armanda Walker   01377 288 416

Wold House, York Road, Fridaythorpe,
Driffield, East Yorkshire YO25 4LD

E: walkerrebori@aol.com
W: www.rebori.com

A family run company based in the Yorkshire Wolds. Rebori has created a unique and diverse range of high quality dressings using the finest ingredients. Our product range includes Mint, Sicilian, Mustard, Fruit and Granelli. All products are ideal for hot or cold food. 'A delicious taste sensation'.

Hospitality

Hotel and restaurants

00 see food highlight map on page 120

Retailers

Deli and independent grocers

East Yorkshire

6 The Pipe and Glass Inn

James Mackenzie   01430 810 246

West End, South Dalton,
Beverley, East Yorkshire HU17 7PN

E: email@pipeandglass.co.uk
W: www.pipeandglass.co.uk

Award winning 18th century country Inn situated in the heart of East Yorkshire. Snug bar and stylish restaurant area, serving modern British food with East Riding accent, wide range of Yorkshire real ales and bespoke wine list.

Winner of Deliciouslyorkshire Best Use of Local Produce in a Menu 2006.

Tickton Grange

David Nowell   01964 543 666

Main Street, Tickton,
Near Beverley, East Yorkshire HU17 9SH

F: 01964 542 556
E: info@ticktongrange.co.uk
W: www.ticktongrange.co.uk

Tickton Grange lies three miles from historic Beverley.

Our two AA rosette Champagne restaurant offers guests a feast of local food from the finest RFGYH producers.

Rhubarb to asparagus, cider to pheasant our menus change seasonally. Our renowned marbled cheese trolley includes 20 regional cheeses, local honey and Yorkshire brack.

2 Costello's Ltd

01377 241 980

55 Market Place, Driffield,
East Yorkshire YO25 6AW

F: 01377 241 980
E: jamescostello@costello-s.com
W: www.costello-s.com

Costello's is a family run craft bakery based in Driffield- capital of the Yorkshire Wolds. We pride ourselves on using traditional methods & recipes that have been passed down through generations of our family, since the 1800's. All of our baking is done by hand & rolling pin - no machines. All of our ingredients are sourced as local as possible. Our pies, quiches, cakes & fruit loaves have a quality well recognised by the food industry due to the numerous awards achievevd from the Guild of Fine Foods - Great Taste Awards. At Costello's, speciality foods have been in the family tradition for over 130 years!

Retailers

00 see food highlight map on page 120

Deli and independent grocers

Morley's of Swanland

Morley Hackford   01482 634 225

12A Westend, Swanland, North Ferriby,
East Riding of Yorkshire HU14 3PE

E: gf@glutenfreebutcher.co.uk
W: www.glutenfreebutcher.co.uk

High class establishment, gluten free sausages, pork pies, steak pies & many more, outdoor reared pigs, Aberdeen Angus stockists, Herdwick Mutton, own curred gammons & bacon, Morleys of Swanland.

Farm shops

1 Burton Agnes Hall Farmer's Food Store

Simon Cunliffe-Lister   01262 490 324

Burton Agnes Hall Courtyard, Driffield,
East Yorkshire YO25 4NB

F: 01262 490 678
W: www.burtonagnes.com

Fresh, seasonal and high quality produce from local farmers. All our food is sourced from Yorkshire farmers and food producers, reducing food miles and supporting local farms and businesses.

Burton Agnes Hall and its award winning gardens are open 11am until 5pm, (please check for times from January - April.) Entrance to the farm shop and the other courtyard shops and cafe is free.

3 Kelleythorpe Farm Shop

Tiffy Hopper   01377 256 627

Kelleythorpe Farm, Driffield,
East Yorkshire YO25 9DW

F: 01377 232 956
E: hoppertiffy@hotmail.com
W: www.kelleythorpefarmshop.co.uk

We specialise in tender, well hung, homebred Aberdeen Angus beef finished traditionally with no additives. Our Angus burgers are legendary.

We also sell a full butchery range of local meats, local vegetables and fruit in season, freshly baked pies and cakes and a good range of English cheeses and other local products.

East Yorkshire

Heartily

deliciouslyyorkshire

135

Retailers

00 see food highlight map on page 120

Distributors

Farm shops

Langlands Farm Shop

Robert Ducker 01430 873 426

York Road, Shiptonthorpe,
York, East Yorkshire YO43 3PN

F: 01430 871 160
E: sales@langlandsgardencentre.co.uk
W: www.langlandsgardencentre.co.uk

Langlands Farm Shop sells the very best locally produced food. In fact, some of it is so local we produce it ourselves! The Farmshop is also filled with tasty treats from the freshest vegetables, through to fresh meats and a huge range of canned treats and hand made chocolates.

4 Manor Farm Shop

Helen Stones 01377 271 038

Hutton Cranswick, Driffield,
East Yorkshire YO25 9PQ

F: 01377 271 038
E: adrian.manorfarm@virgin.net

Established for over 17 years we are a family run shop employing local people, selling local food. Mouthwatering produce including made to order sandwiches, over 40 British cheeses, home cooked meats, quality fruit & veg and fabulous Yorkshire ice cream, from cornets to takeaway tubs. Plus much more.

Open Mon-Fri 9.00am-6.00pm, Sat 9.00am-5.00pm, Sun 10.00am-4.00pm

Hider Foods Imports Ltd

David Hider 01482 561 137

Wiltshire Road, Kingston-upon-Hull,
East Yorkshire HU4 6PA

F: 01482 565 668
E: david@hiderfoods.co.uk
W: www.hiderfoods.co.uk

Hider Food Imports Limited are a family owned company, specialising in quality food, be that Nuts & Dried Fruits or the very best delicatessen products from around the world.

Local, continental, organic, fair-trade, gluten-free . . . and much more in stock.

We cover the country with our own fleet of lorries, giving a friendly, weekly delivery service supplying the best confectionery, cakes, biscuits and fruit available to man.

Try us once and join the family.

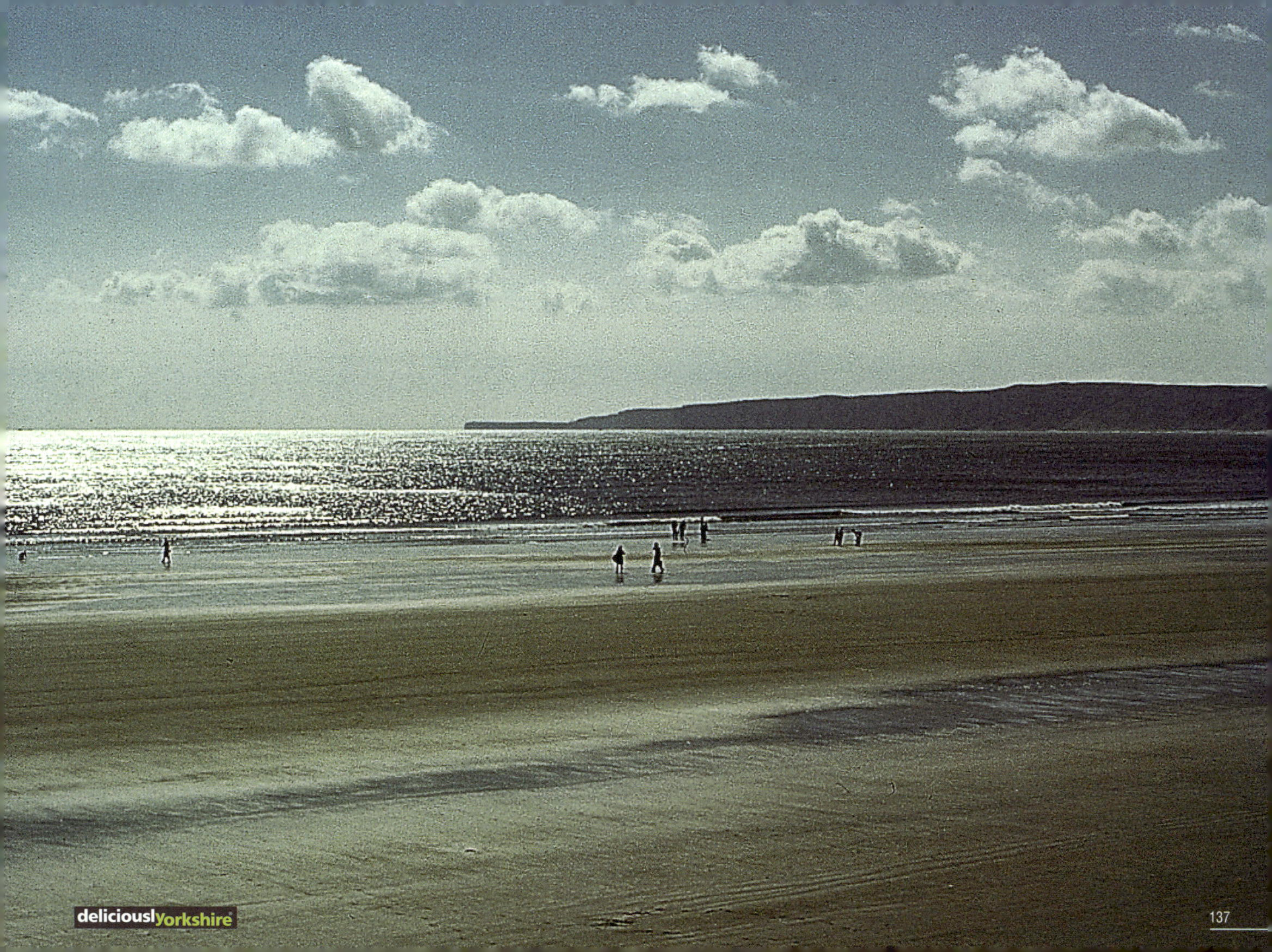

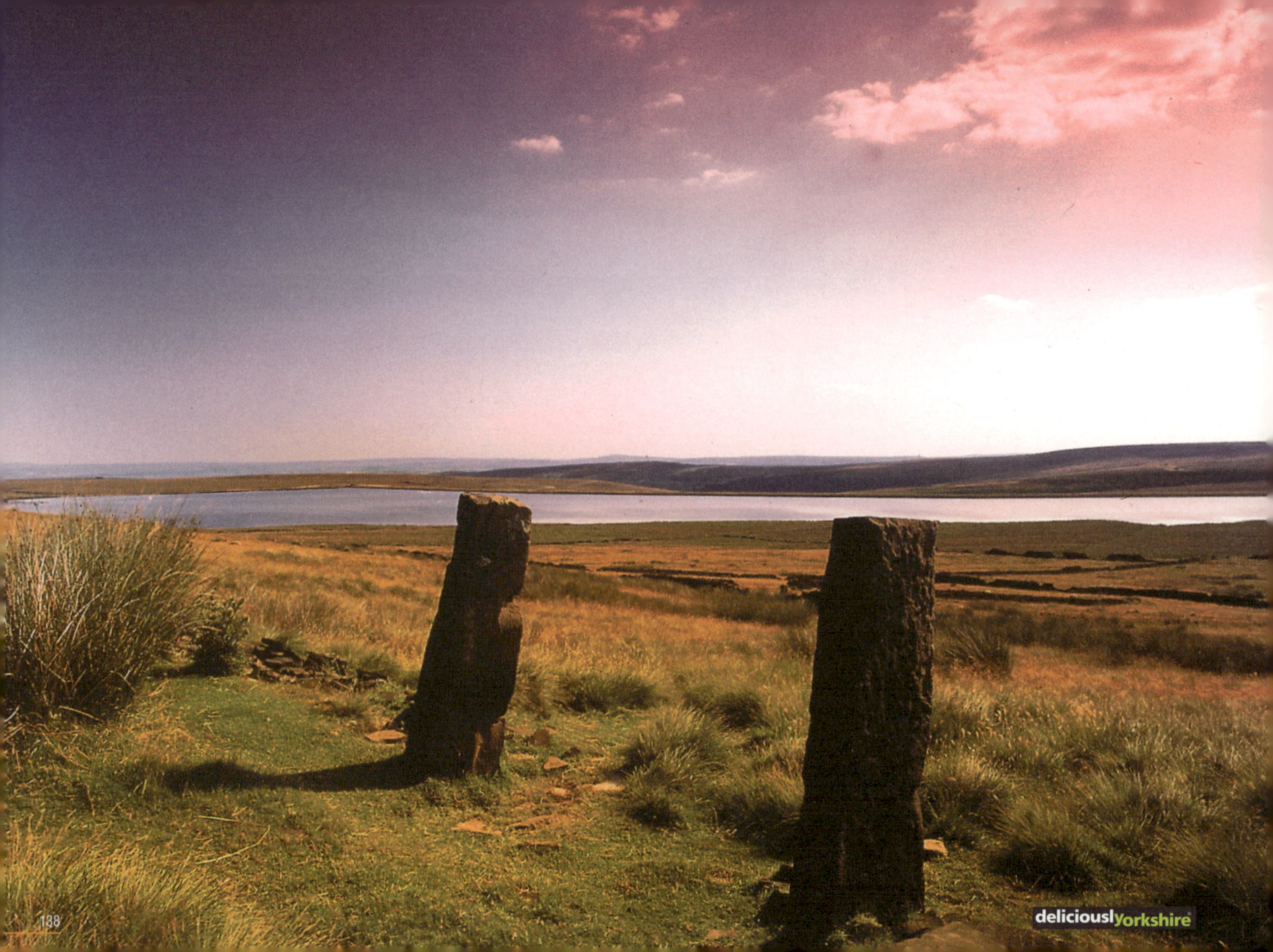

West Yorkshire

West Yorkshire – shopping heaven or wild wilderness?

Both – and everything in between. While moors and mines were vital ingredients in West Yorkshire life, it is wool that shaped the landscape and its development most dramatically.

Perfectly situated with ideal pasture for sheep, fast-flowing streams and rivers and a youthful, hard working population, towns such as Leeds, Halifax and Holmfirth grew rich. Long since silenced, the mills now play host to art galleries, craft spaces, museums and restaurants.

This big bountiful region offers lush landscapes, glorious people of rare warmth and individuality, coupled with historic sites and innovative attractions.

With a vibrant shopping centre based around the magnificent Victoria Quarter and Harvey Nichols, pavement cafes and cutting edge boutiques – Leeds has it all for the most demanding of shoppers. Culturally diverse and innovative Bradford offers some of the finest curries in the world, along with the award-winning National Media Museum.

A rich cultural heritage enables visitors to explore the formidable fortresses of kings, queens and conquerors and the spiritual harmony of the greatest abbeys in the north. Visit the parsonage at the Brontes Haworth and tread the vast lonely moor which inspired the sweeping romance of Wuthering Heights or Holmfirth, popular with lovers of Last of the Summer Wine. Alternatively travel back to a by-gone era on the steam-driven Keighley and Worth Valley Railway.

West Yorkshire

West Yorkshire Food Highlights

Useful contacts

www.deliciouslyyorkshire.co.uk
www.yorkshire.com
www.leedsliveitloveit.com
www.visitbradford.com
www.leeds.gov.uk
www.barnsley.gov.uk
www.calderdale.gov.uk
www.kirklees.gov.uk
www.wakefield.gov.uk

1 Blacker Hall Farm Shop
Farm shop (see entry on p160)

2 Holdsworth House
Hotel and restaurant (see entry on p182)

3 The Old Registry
Guest house (see entry on p184)

4 Yummy Yorkshire Ice Cream Company
Ice cream shop (see entry on p150)

5 Watermill Restaurant (Milford Hotel)
Restaurant (see entry on p185)

6 Wilsons of Crossgates
Butcher (see entry on p154)

7 Keelham Hall Farm Shop
Farm shop (see entry on p161)

deliciouslyorkshire

Shops local – Bradford

A world heritage site*, an Internationally-Celebrated Artist, much-loved authors and the National Museum for Media: just a few headlines about much-maligned Bradford. It's not all bad for a city that has been through its fair share of ups and downs.

But of course, one of the defining elements of modern Bradford is the melting pot of cultures, which together make for a food lover's heaven. From Britain's finest curries to locally-produced pork pies, Bradford's industrious history can still be seen today in the number of food businesses thriving in and around the city.

Visit **www.deliciouslyorkshire.co.uk** to look for other producers. Here's a pick of the best.

*That's Sir Titus Salt's 'model' Victorian village Saltaire, now a UNESCO World Heritage Site. Salt's Mill itself is now a gallery, housing a collection of the works of internationally-celebrated artist David Hockney, who was born in Bradford.

West Yorkshire

Brazilian Flavours

Even a decade in Yorkshire doesn't qualify you as a local – but marrying a Yorkshireman and becoming a leading light of the Deliciouslyorkshire network helps.

Isabel Gordon's cheese bread, Pão de Queijo, may not have its roots in this country, but its heart definitely resides here.

Launched only a year ago – but already proving a big hit – the snacks are gluten and wheat free, low in salt, and free from artificial colour and preservatives. Sold frozen and ready-to-bake into a meltingly cheesy treat, Pão de Queijo makes a delicious snack for both adults and children. But watch out – the aroma of those little morsels warming up in the oven is irresistible!

Look out for more authentic Brazilian foods launching soon, including superfruit salad dressings packed with vitamins, taste and vibrant colours!

West Yorkshire

Denholme Gate Apiary

It's the very fabric of Yorkshire that makes Denholme Gate's honey what it is.

The hives are situated in different areas, creating very different products. There's a pale, creamy spring blossom honey, a delicate-tasting borage honey, a rich, golden summer flower honey and a strong, dark honey from the heather moors.

You can even buy honey on the comb, as well as associated beeswax products. No wonder Denholme Gate was nominated as one of UKTV Food's 'food heroes'.

John Lord & Sons 'Take & Bake'

In his early 60s, as most of his contemporaries are contemplating retirement, butcher John Lord is just embarking on an entirely new venture – posh pies.

The high quality pies, made from local ingredients, have just been given a big thumbs up by the Yorkshire Pork Pie Appreciation Society, which awarded them an 'unheard-of' full marks in two categories.

The USP is that the pies are of premium quality and they're not pre-cooked and sitting around on a shelf – they're sold frozen to be cooked at home, or in the restaurant kitchen. Although they can be enjoyed at room temperature, John wants to remind customers of the joys of eating the pies warm from the oven.

John said: "What we're trying to do is to recreate the old days when people used to queue outside the butcher's shop and eat pork pies fresh from the oven, with the gravy dribbling down their chins."

West Yorkshire

Keelham Hall Farm Shop

A genuinely family-run business, Keelham Hall Farm Shop specialises in its own homemade sausages and home cooked hams – and in friendly, knowledgeable, personal service.

Really several separate shops within a shop, it also sells fresh seasonal fruit and veg a plenty, plus fresh flowers and plants, beer and wine, eggs, cheese and dairy products and even pet food and cupboard essentials. Keelham Hall prides itself in stocking everything you need for the weekly shop.

Love Bites Sandwiches

Another Bradford family business, Love Bites offers you the world within two slices of bread – or a bagel, a roll, some ciabatta, on a pizza, in a panini etc etc.

With a dazzling range of world flavours as fillings, the 50-strong workforce even puts together Halal and 'waistwatcher' ranges. They're best-known in the area as the people to call for a buffet platter for that important meeting, celebration or party.

The Real Bradford Curry Company

The man who helped to build the internationally successful Harry Ramsden's brand has teamed up with a Bradfordian who's passionate about South Asian cuisine and culture to create this venture, which delivers real Bradford curries to the nation's doorstep.

Business marketing guru Richard Richardson and Bradford businesswoman Jan Smithies scoured the city to find the best restaurants, home cooks and caterers. These people – the 'Curry Heroes' – have helped create an innovative menu which really reflects the diversity and vibrancy of South Asian cooking.

Meals are handmade in small batches from the highest quality ingredients. They are then instantly flash frozen to preserve them without the need for additives, packed and delivered to the customer's door by overnight courier.

Seabrook Crisps

Never mind those ubiquitous snacks promoted by a certain footballer, Seabrooks are the crisp of choice for the North – and they're still made in Bradford.

Established more than 60 years ago, today's company may manufacture 18 different flavours, but the team is just as dedicated as their founder to creating Britain's tastiest crisps. For Yorkshire tykes feeling peckish, nothing else will do.

West Yorkshire

deliciously Yorkshire

Shops local – Ilkley

Such is the fame of the song about Ilkley Moor that unfortunate Southerners probably envisage any nearby dwelling-place as some kind of muddy, down at heel Yorkshire village, far removed from reasonable civilisation.

We can live with that – because it leaves the rest of us free to enjoy the many delights of this elegant spa town, including its breathtaking surrounding countryside, one of the nation's few remaining lidos, exciting shopping, great hotels and, most importantly of all, some really excellent local food. Despite Ilkley's size, the town has carved out a big reputation as a foodie destination.

Ilkley may be rather smart now but its reputation is built on firm Yorkshire foundations. Unnecessary flounces and frivolities aren't welcome here. Rather, Ilkley has taken the traditional Yorkshire foodie elements and honed them to perfection.

Thus, you'll find one of the world-famous Bettys tea rooms, a real, high class butcher and the kind of pub you thought only existed in your dreams.

It's got everything you need for a delicious weekend away – whether you have to travel hundreds of miles to get there or just a few minutes.

Bettys and Taylors

This world-famous institution, with its strangely successful blend of Swiss/Yorkshire cooking, needs little introduction.

Whether you pop in for tea and a 'fat rascal' (if you don't know what it is yet, you'd better try one) or a full evening meal, you'll find proper old-fashioned service and excellent food, created from fresh ingredients which are often sourced locally.

And there's a seductive shop so full of goodies and gifts that it defies you to leave empty-handed.

Lishman's of Ilkley

David Lishman's butcher's shop is a genuine class act. With a list of awards as long as its famous strings of sausages, David was even singled out as one of Rick Stein's food heroes.

David is passionate about Yorkshire – sourcing all his meat from the county and popping a fair few other local goodies on the shelves. The team also makes a point of buying rare breed meats, knowing that if there's no demand, these animals will simply die out. These are butchers who know their suppliers personally, enabling them to hand-pick the meat, confident about the entire process, from field to plate.

West Yorkshire

Ilkley Moor Vaults

Known locally as 'The Taps', this recently renovated pub is the kind of place you'd given up hope of finding. It's about good beer, fine wine and fresh, simple, seasonal food made from top-quality ingredients.

If the words 'pub menu' conjure up images of reheated lasagne, you're in for a surprise. Everything here is home made, from the sourdough bread to the chips and the ice cream.

Lunch could be an organic chicken sandwich with tarragon mayonnaise, or perhaps beef and 'Old Peculiar' (a local beer) pie. The dinner menu may offer duck breast and roast parsnips with honey or a rib-eye steak from neighbouring Lishman's butchers. And there's also serious food for the under 12s, with choices such as organic chicken, chips and salad that will keep both the mini-munchers and their parents happy.

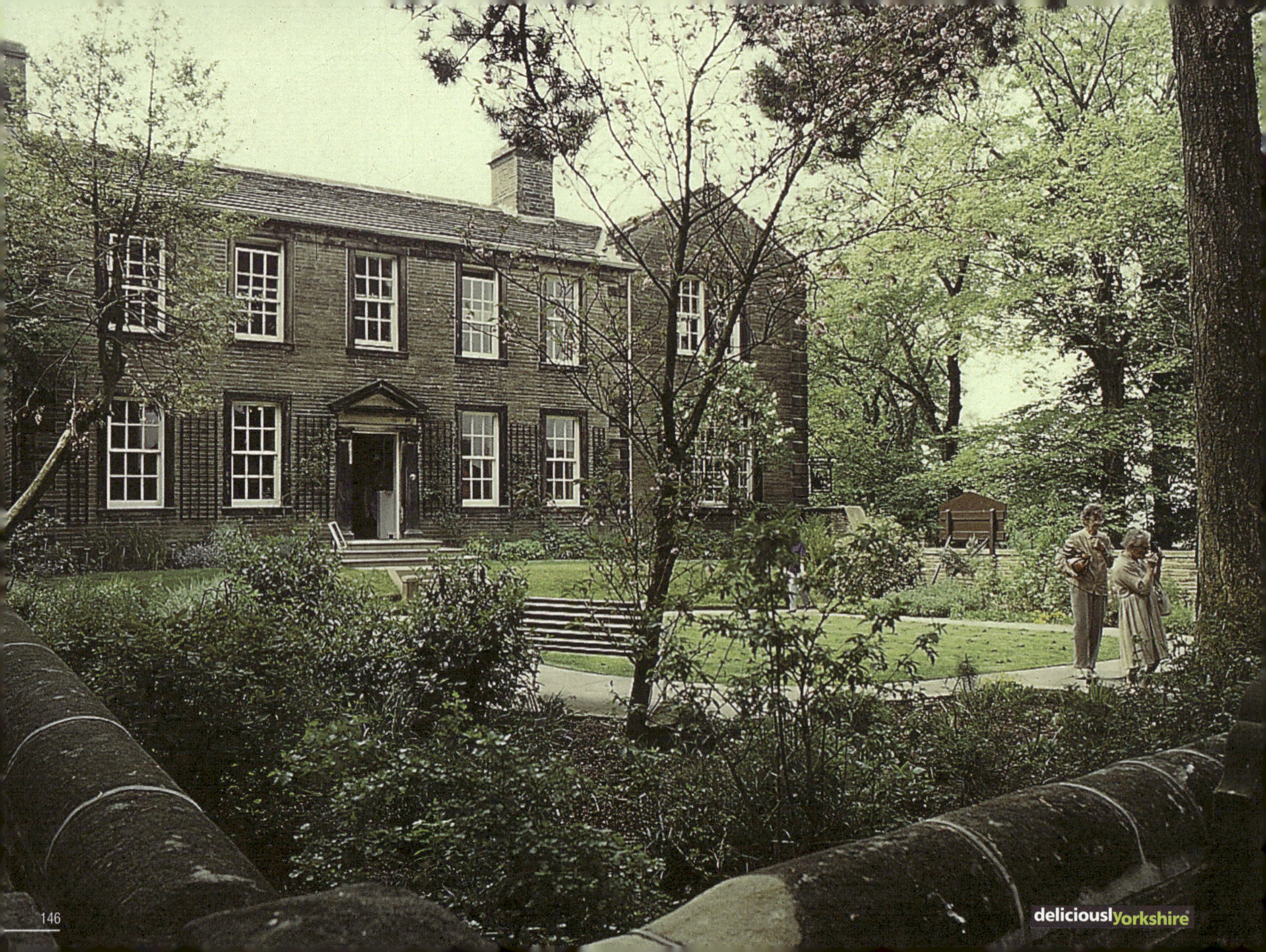

West Yorkshire Members

deliciouslyyorkshire

Producers

Bakers and confectioners

West Yorkshire

Bagel Nash

Karen Mizrahi 01132 930 393

Buslingthorpe Green, Meanwood,
Leeds, West Yorkshire LS7 2HG

E: karen@bagelnash.com
W: www.bagelnash.com

Bagel Nash specialise in producing the tastiest bagels using the finest quality ingredients. We are dedicated to ensuring that all our products are completely wholesome with no additives or preservatives. They are also virtually fat and cholesterol free.

Grandma Wilds Biscuits

John Bateman 01535 650 500

The Bakery, Millenium Business Park, Station Road, Steeton, Keighley, West Yorkshire BD20 6RB

F: 01535 650 509
E: sales@grandma-wilds.co.uk
W: www.grandma-wilds.co.uk

Grandma Wilds award winning biscuits baked on trays, ensuring wholesome, crunchy biscuits baked without compromise in the traditional way.

Johnson's Toffees

Tony Johnson 01977 515 961

Carrwood Road, Glasshoughton,
Castleford, West Yorkshire WF10 4SB

F: 01977 515 961

Johnsons Toffees is a family run business, with over 70 years experience manufacturing quality confectionary. Only the finest ingredients are used to produce creamy caramel toffees and a vast selection of fudges and truffles. As we manufacture all of our own products we can guarantee a consistent high standard, using traditional methods.

Deliciously

deliciouslyYorkshire

Producers

Bakers and confectioners

Ridings of Yorkshire

Peter Gledhill   01422 888 050

Unit 1, Orchard Business Park, Mytholmroyd,
Halifax, West Yorkshire HX7 5HZ

E: info@ridingsofyorkshire.com
W: www.ridingsofyorkshire.com

At Ridings of Yorkshire we are dedicated to building your business via a range of superior baked goods based on traditional recipes and using superior ingredients.

The Helen Francis Cake Company

Helen Willmot   07722 881 821

35 Bankfield Terrace, Burley,
Leeds, West Yorkshire LS4 2RE

E: sales@helenfranciscupcakes.co.uk
W: www.helenfranciscupcakes.co.uk

The Helen Francis Cake Company makes delicious, exquisite handmade and decorated cupcakes, using the finest quality ingredients. The cupcakes are made to order, elegantly presented and delivered to your door.

Dairy and eggs

Charlottes Jersey Ice Cream Ltd

Geoffery Wraithmell   01924 494 491

The Meadows, Lane Top Farm, Whitley,
Dewsbury, West Yorkshire WF12 0NQ

F: 01924 498 092
E: info@charlottesjerseyicecream.co.uk
W: www.charlottesjerseyicecream.co.uk

Our herd of Jersey cows produces the milk & double cream used in our luxury artisan dairy ice cream, with natural ingredients & comes in 24 flavours.

Organic Dales

Steven Lofthouse   01943 463 044

Scow Hall Farm, Norwood,
Otley, West Yorkshire LS21 2QX

F: 01943 463 044
E: stevenlofthouse@hotmail.com
W: www.organicdales.co.uk

Organic Dales and Clever Cow Organics produce and supply Yorkshire certified-organic pasteurised milk and cream to shops, schools, bakeries and restaurants, in all the usual sizes of containers, for use or resale and 13.6 litre pergals.

Organic Dales delivers in a refrigerated trailer and van, within the local area.

West Yorkshire

Producers

00 see food highlight map on page 140

Dairy and eggs

4 Yummy Yorkshire Ice Cream Company (P. Holmes & Son)

Jeremy Holmes   01226 762 551

Delph House Farm, Denby,
Huddersfield, West Yorkshire HD8 8XY

- F: 01226 762 888
- E: jeremyholmes@farmersweekly.net
- W: www.yorkshiremilk.co.uk

Delph House Farm dairy, the home of 'yorkshiremilk.co.uk' and 'Yummy Yorkshire Ice Cream Company' produce high quality milk, cream and ice cream from a Friesian Holstein herd. Yummy Yorkshire is made using natural ingredients to retain the true essence of each flavour. Available direct from the farm or through local retailers.

Beverages – alcoholic and non alcoholic

Lemon Tree

Andrew Kay   01484 686 826

26 Victoria Street, Holmfirth,
West Yorkshire HD9 7DE

- E: andrewkay69@tiscali.co.uk

The Lemon Tree Fresh Lemonade Bar produces hand pressed, freshly squeezed, lemonade, made to order and is served by the cup, ice cold. The company currently operates during the summer season at numerous agricultural shows and events.

Splash Winery Ltd

Paul Vickerman   01484 323 814

16 Briar Avenue, Meltham,
Holmfirth, West Yorkshire HD9 5LQ

- E: paul@splashwines.com
- W: www.splashwines.com

Set in the shadows of the Pennines of Yorkshire, Splash Winery produce wines from top quality fruit, flowers & berries & naturally soft Pennine water.

Yorkshire Hills

Phillip Tinker   01484 683 468

Scholes Moor, Holmfirth,
Huddersfield, West Yorkshire HD9 1RU

- F: 01484 683 468
- E: yhsw47@hotmail.com
- W: www.yorkshirehillsspringwater.co.uk

Yorkshire Hills Spring Water is a family owned business based in the heart of Yorkshire, England, where we produce high quality, natural, refreshing drinks. We produce a range of still and sparkling waters as well as flavoured waters.

Juicer is a uniquely tasting natural product made with natural spring water blended with exotic fruit juices. With no additives, preservatives or stabilisers, Juicer is popular as a healthy drink in restaurants, pubs, wine bars, fitness centres, delicatessens, colleges, health stores and other outlets.

Producers

Fresh ingredients

D. Westwood & Son

David/Jonathan Westwood 01924 822 314

Thorpe Lane, Thorpe, Wakefield,
West Yorkshire WF3 3BZ

F: 01924 870 668
E: dwsthorpefarms@btconnect.com
W: www.dwsyorkshireboxes.co.uk

A large variety of crops are grown such as rhubarb, cauliflower, broccoli and a variety of cabbages.

The specialist rhubarb crop is grown in the heart of the famous Yorkshire Rhubarb Triangle.

All the products are supplied loose or pre-packed as required by the customer. Contact Westwood's for further information.

E. Oldroyd & Sons Ltd

Janet Oldroyd Hulme 01132 822 245

Hopefield Farm, Leadwell Lane,
Rothwell, Leeds, West Yorkshire LS26 0ST

F: 01132 828 775
E: eoldroyd@btconnect.com
W: www.yorkshirerhubarb.co.uk

A family owned company producing and packing high quality fruit and vegetables.

The company has a high media profile, being one of the countries largest producers of rhubarb, having 5 generations experience in traditionally grown winter rhubarb. Many celebrity chefs have made visits to the Oldroyd's due to the resurgence in popularity of this traditional crop. Janet Oldroyd Hulme has become affectionately known by the media as the 'High Priestess of Rhubarb'.

The company is listed as a Rick Stein Food Hero Producer.

W S Bentley (Growers) Ltd

Jan Bentley 01274 851 214

Cliffe Hill Nurseries, Cliffe Lane,
Gomersal, West Yorkshire BD19 4SX

F: 01274 851 213
E: enquires@wsbentley.co.uk
W: www.saladcress.co.uk

W S Bentley (Growers) Ltd, Specialist Salad Cress growers of Gomersal supplying two of the major multiples nationwide, ready to introduce sprouted seeds into the retail, catering and processing market. Investors in People, BRC and Assured Produce accredited.

Famously

West Yorkshire

Producers

Ingredient suppliers

Gordon Rhodes & Son

Jayne Horrocks 01274 758 000

Dalesman House, Chaseway,
Bradford, West Yorkshire BD5 8HW

- **F:** 01274 758 009
- **E:** jayne.horrocks@thedalesmangroup.co.uk
- **W:** www.thedalesmangroup.co.uk

Gordon Rhodes & Son is a Grade A, BRC Certified seasoning manufacturer, producing bespoke flavours for the meat, fish and bakery industries.

The product portfolio contains over 3000 recipes - sausage and burger seasonings, stuffing, black pudding, sauce and gravy mixes, pie and pasty seasonings, curing compounds, glazes and coaters.

Ulrick & Short

Andrew Ulrick 01977 620 011

Walton Wood Farm, Thorpe Audlin,
Pontefract, West Yorkshire WF8 3HG

- **F:** 01977 620 022
- **E:** us@ulrickandshort.com
- **W:** www.ulrickandshort.com

Ulrick & Short supply clean label functional food ingredients, which are completely free from chemical, enzymic or genetic modification. We specialise in ingredients for bakery, processed meats, sauces and coatings.

Meat, poultry and game – fresh and smoked

Far Isle Farm (Formerly S&C Meats)

Chris Argent 01422 244 859

259 Shay Lane, Holmfield,
Halifax, West Yorkshire HX2 9AG

- **F:** 01422 246 343
- **E:** info@farislefarm.co.uk
- **W:** www.farislefarm.co.uk

Welcome to Far Isle Farm - a family run business.

Naturally reared meats are our speciality. With over 30 years experinece on the farm and in the farm shop, we can offer a full range of hand made sausages, poultry, beef, lamb, dry cured bacon and game.

Mail order service available.

Producers

Meat, poultry and game – fresh and smoked

Lishman's of Ilkley (York Ham & Sausage Co.)

David Lishman   01943 609 436

23-27 Leeds Road, Ilkley,
West Yorkshire LS29 8DP

- **F:** 01943 603 809
- **E:** david@lishmansofilkley.co.uk
- **W:** www.lishmansofilkley.co.uk

High quality traditional butchers producing home cured hams, bacon, championship sausage and black puddings, using livestock born and bred in Yorkshire.

Specially
deliciously yorkshire

Pies

Andrew Jones Pies

Andrew Jones   01484 548 137

14 Old Leeds Road,
Huddersfield, West Yorkshire HD1 1SP

- **F:** 01484 548 138
- **E:** info@piesandpastries.co.uk
- **W:** www.jones-butchers.co.uk

Award winning pie makers selling to farm shops, delis, butchers, sports clubs and bakeries etc, with a freshly baked range delivered daily or a range of pies to bake off.

J. Lord & Son 'Take & Bake' Ltd

Jonny Lord   08456 860 331

6 Thorn Avenue, Heaton,
Bradford, West Yorkshire BD9 6LS

- **F:** 01612 361 980
- **E:** jonny@jlordandson.co.uk
- **W:** www.jlordanndson.co.uk

We have one simple mission, to restore the humble pork pie to its rightful place in the hearts and minds of ordinary folk. Traditional pork pies of all shapes and sizes plus alternative fillings and bespoke pies made to order. Availability - Factory door, Farmers Markets, Selected outlets.

West Yorkshire

153

Producers

00 see food highlight map on page 140

Pies

Pie & Ltd

Craig Blick   07789 214 357

Keighley Business Centre, South Street,
Keighley, West Yorkshire BD21 1AG

- **E:** craig@pieand.co.uk

Pie & supply individually packaged quality pies to various outlets, including Delicatessens, Cafés, Pubs and Sports clubs. 'Pie &' pies are free from additives and preservatives, yet they are full of flavour.

The Crusty Pie Company

Diane Congreve   01274 673 664

Liongate House Bakery, Stanage Lane, Shelf,
Halifax, West Yorkshire HX3 7PR

- **F:** 01274 673 664
- **E:** diane@crustypie.co.uk
- **W:** www.crustypie.co.uk

Traditional and speciality pies, pasties and sausage rolls, sold with our own range of delicious chutney.

The Denby Dale Pie Company

Janet Purcell   01484 862 585

Unit 12 Denby Dale Business Park, Wakefield Road,
Denby Dale, Huddersfield, West Yorkshire HD8 8QH

- **F:** 01484 863 006
- **E:** enquires@denbydalepiecompany.co.uk
- **W:** www.denbydalepiecompany.co.uk

The Denby Dale Pie Company started trading in the village of Denby Dale which is steeped in pie tradition and famous as the 'Pie capital of the World' where the world's largest pie was baked. Our objective is to provide high quality frozen meat pies. Using traditional methods, hand made from preperation to finishing, including the best quality ingredients such as chuck steak. Our measure of success is when we are described as "LOOKS HOME-MADE" and "TASTES HOME-MADE".

6 Wilsons of Crossgates

John and Andrew Green   01132 645 448

38 Austhorpe Road, Crossgates,
Leeds, West Yorkshire LS15 8DX

- **F:** 01132 930 516
- **E:** john@wilsonsbutchers.co.uk
- **W:** www.wilsonsbutchers.co.uk

Wilsons, "Englands Best Butchers 2005 -2006", are situated on the outskirts of Leeds close to the A1-M1 link. Specialities include their triple award winning Pork Pies, Yorkshire's best thin pork sausage, extra mature beef, free range pork and traditional home cooked meats. A hidden gem with it's friendly knowledgeable staff and mouth-watering displays.

West Yorkshire

154

Producers

Prepared food

Areolives

Nick Taylor 01937 844 600

422a Thorpe Arch Estate, Wetherby,
West Yorkshire LS23 7BJ

F: 01937 845 600
E: sales@areolives.com
W: www.areolives.com

Traditional Greek marinated olives and olive oil
- Gold winning olives imported direct from Greece
- Marinades created fresh to order in house
- Olives are packed into a range of sizes in our production unit near Wetherby
- Over 10 tonnes of olives so all requirements can be met
- BRC accreditation

For further information contact Areolives on 01937 844600

Brazilian Flavours

Isabel Gordon 08712 313 399

Commerce Court, Challenge Way, Cutler Heights Lane,
Bradford, West Yorkshire BD4 8NW

E: bel@brazilianflavours.net
W: www.brazilianflavours.net

We produce high-quality, clean label, innovative and authentic Brazilian foods, using only the finest ingredients, all made in Yorkshire. Our current range includes speciality cheesebreads (gluten & wheat - free, ready-to-bake from frozen), superfruit tropical jams (including cashew fruit, acai and guava), and superfruit salad dressings, packed with vitamins, taste and vibrant colours!

Love Bites Foods

John Varey 01274 627 000

Granary Court, Eccleshill,
Bradford, West Yorkshire BD2 2EF

F: 01274 627 627
E: enquiries@love-bites.co.uk
W: www.love-bites.co.uk

For over a decade multi award winning Love Bites have been creating and distributing premium chilled food products to a variety of clients, from the NHS to leading sports stadiums, Airlines to the nation's favourite high street supermarkets. Our BRC quality accredited ranges include both our own and private labels of the following; Sandwiches, pizzas, paninis, salads, function platters and microwavable food to go.

"Magnificent food and so much more"

West Yorkshire

deliciouslyorkshire

Producers

Prepared food

Seabrook Crisps Ltd

Roger Gladman   01274 546 405

Seabrook House, Duncombe Street, Ingleby Road, Bradford, West Yorkshire BD8 9AJ

F: 01274 542 235
E: rogerg@seabrookcrisps.com
W: www.seabrookcrisps.com

Seabrook are the North's best-loved crisps. They've always been known for their full flavour, crunch and purer ingredients – like sunflower oil and sea salt and now all 18 flavours are free from nasties like MSG.

Heartily

Soup Dragons (Bon Bouche)

Jo Sykes   01924 339 700

Bon Bouche, 8a Thompsons Yard, Wakefield, West Yorkshire WF1 2TP

F: 01924 339 622
E: bonbouchecatering@tiscali.co.uk

We're not really dragons; we just have a fiery passion for soup. Hand made with only one thing in mind - great taste. Using only quality fresh produce from local suppliers, seasoned with organic herbs and spices our soups are very low in fat. **Vegetarian and vegan friendly**, they contain no wheat so are suitable for many types of diets. Fresh from the kitchens of the Soup Dragons. Enjoy...

The Real Bradford Curry Company

Jan Smithies   07947 139 066/08452 574 260

Think Business, Richmond Road, Bradford, West Yorkshire BD7 1DP

E: jan@realbradfordcurry.com
W: www.realbradfordcurry.com

Authentic Bradford curries direct to your doorstep - anywhere in mainland UK. Choose from our great range of starters & curries on our secure, accessible website.

We can have your order delivered to you within two working days. Great for parties, sharing with friends, or filling up your freezer to 'dine out at home'.

'We're nearly in tears here the food is so good!' Radio 2 Drive Time review.

West Yorkshire

deliciouslyyorkshire

Producers

Prepared food

Zeina Foods Ltd

Chris Fahy   01924 280 180

Milner Way, Ossett, Wakefield,
West Yorkshire WF5 9JE

F: 01924 280 559
E: sales@zeinafoods.com
W: www.zeinafoods.com

Zeina Foods is an established family business specialising in nuts, dried fruit and chocolate products. True to our passion for tasty and healthy food, we offer high quality, award winning brands such as **NUTZ and Flavours of the World**. We are BRC accredited offering excellent customer service for both wholesale and retail customers.

Preserves, honey, condiments and spices

Curry Cuisine

Paresh Tejura   07952 112 810

3 Turnberry Drive, Tingley,
West Yorkshire WF3 1AQ

E: enquiries@currycuisine.co.uk
W: www.currycuisine.co.uk

Curry Cuisine have created a range of blended spice mixes and pickles based on traditional Gujarati recipes passed down through generations. Each mix includes a recipe and step by step instructions. Curry Cuisine also offers authentic Indian cookery courses and demonstration evenings showing you how cooking Indian food is fun and exciting.

Denholme Gate Apiary

Liz Joyce   01274 835 490

The Gatehouse, Brighouse Road, Denholme Gate, Bradford, West Yorkshire BD13 4EP

F: 01274 835 490
E: liz@denholmegatehoney.co.uk
W: www.denholmegatehoney.co.uk

Denholme Gate Apiary produces quality honey from the Yorkshire countryside, offering spring blossom, summer flower, golden borage and heather moorlands.

Honey all in 340g jars, and honeycomb in 225g boxes.

Naturally

West Yorkshire

deliciouslyyorkshire

Producers

Preserves, honey, condiments and spices

West Yorkshire

Granny's Kitchen

Meg/Dave Cooper   01132 553 884

Unit C1, St Catherines Business Centre, Broad Lane, Bramley, Leeds, West Yorkshire LS13 2TD

F: 01132 393 694

Granny's Kitchen Preserves have been produced since 1987, using traditional methods and recipes.

They contain no preservatives, colourings or flavourings and are suitable for vegetarians & coeliacs as they are also gluten free. Fruits and vegetables are sourced locally- you really should try our fresh fruit marmalade, just like Granny made - only better.

Wharfe Valley Farms

Geoff Kilby   01937 572 084

Jewitt Lane, Collingham,
Wetherby, West Yorkshire LS22 5BA

E: info@wharfevalleyfarms.co.uk
W: www.wharfevalleyfarms.co.uk

Culinary Rapeseed Oil Producers. Our oil is grown, pressed, filtered, bottled and labelled on the Kilby's farm in Collingham in our purpose built press room.

The bottles are available in 250ml and 500ml sizes for retail use and in 5 litre and 20 litre containers for the catering market.

Shaws of Huddersfield Ltd

Daniel Shaw   01484 539 999

Shaw Park Office Centre, Silver Street, Huddersfield, West Yorkshire HD5 9AF

F: 01484 542 709
E: reception@shaws1889.com
W: www.shaws1889.com

An independent family business manufacturing quality chutney, relish, salsa and sauces to both retail and catering customers. There are over 60 to choose from. Which is your favourite?

Womersley Fine Foods Ltd

01977 797 924

18 Beastfair, Pontefract,
West Yorkshire WF8 1AW

F: 01977 780 465
E: sales@womersleyfinefoods.co.uk
W: www.womersleyfinefoods.co.uk

The Womersley brand was launched from Womersley Hall in 1979, and has become one of Yorkshire's and England's leading gourmet brands for fruit vinegars, dressings and jellies, also a new range of marinated olives. Products now available in foodservice size containers.

deliciouslyorkshire

Hospitality

Hotels and restaurants

Ilkley Moor Vaults

Joe or Elizabeth McDermott   01943 607 012

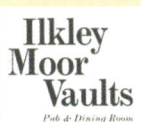

Stockeld Road, Ilkley,
West Yorkshire LS29 9HD

- **E:** info@ilkleymoorvaults.co.uk
- **W:** www.ilkleymoorvaults.co.uk

Opened in 2006, we are a pub serving fresh, seasonal food with real ales & good wines. We are passionate about using top quality ingredients produced with compassion and care. We aim to source as much local, organic and free-range produce as we can to give customers a real taste of Yorkshire. Everything is home-made from our organic sourdough bread to the free-range pork sausages and the ice-creams made with delicious local organic cream. The pub has log fires, an outdoor terrace and is open for lunch, dinner & Sunday lunch.

Thorpe Park Hotel & Spa

Gordon Jackson   01132 641 000

1150 Century Way, Thorpe Park,
Leeds, West Yorkshire LS15 8ZB

- **F:** 01132 641 010
- **E:** thorpepark.gm@shirehotels.co.uk
- **W:** www.shirehotels.com

A contemporary and stylish restaurant, with spacious al fresco terrace for the summer months. Chef Doug Hargreaves works with local suppliers and features seasonal produce on all his menus. AA rosette awarded.

Outside caterers

Boutique Catering

Paul Rowntree   01132 244 811

BOUTIQUE

Carlton Mills, Pickering Street, Armley,
Leeds, West Yorkshire LS12 2QG

- **F:** 01132 310 601
- **E:** enquiries@boutique-catering.co.uk
- **W:** www.boutique-catering.co.uk

Boutique Catering provides bespoke catering experiences for any event or occasion.

We specialise in event catering, private dining, parties, product launches, barbecues, boardroom lunches and venue sourcing.

Led by Michelin trained chef Paul Rowntree, our team always delivers the highest quality serivce whatever the occasion or budget.

West Yorkshire

deliciouslyorkshire

Hospitality

Outside caterers

Cucina

Steve Quinn   08453 891 320

Poplar Farm, Notton,
West Yorkshire WF4 2NQ

F: 08453 891 321
E: steve@cucina.co.uk
W: www.cucina.co.uk

Cucina are a specialist Contract Caterer setting new benchmarks in businesses and schools in England. A fast growing company, we work with partners who require good food served with flair. We offer clients: significant increases in useage as customers want to eat with us; the use of fresh, local ingredients; a 'stealthy approach' to eating whereby goodness is hidden in popular food; cookery in front of our customers; innovative menus (linked to the curriculum in schools); a highly personalised service to meet customers needs and energy and enthusiasm is evident in all areas of our service.

Retailers

Deli and independent grocers

Cryer & Stott

Richard Holmes   01977 511 022

5 Weir View, Castleford,
West Yorkshire WF10 2SF

E: info@cryerandstott.co.uk
W: www.cryerandstott.co.uk

At Cryer & Stott Cheese Mongers our aim is simple, to be the premier merchant of Yorkshire cheese and produce. Cryer & Stott own three deli shops. Named in the top 15 cheese merchants by 'The Independent' newspaper. Consultant to Channel 4 television. Named 'Business of the Year' by 'The Regional Food Group for Yorkshire and Humber'. Producer of Ruby Gold the worlds' only rhubarb cheese, which won a gold medal at the Nantwich Cheese Awards.

00 see food highlight map on page 140

Farm shops

1 Blacker Hall Farm Shop

01924 267 202

Branch Road, Calder Grove,
Wakefield, West Yorkshire WF4 3DN

F: 01924 263 849
E: info@blackerhall.com
W: www.blackerhall.com

At Blacker Hall Farm Shop over 90% of the food we sell is produced or prepared on the premises. The butchery, bakery and delicatessen offer a wide range of award winning local produce. Meat from our own farm and other neighbouring farms. Best Farm Shop in England (Meat Trades Journal).

West Yorkshire

160

deliciously yorkshire

Retailers

00 see food highlight map on page 140

Farm shops

Farmer Copleys

Heather Copley 01977 600 200

Ravensknowle Farm, Pontefract Road, Purston, West Yorkshire WF7 5AF

E: info@farmercopleys.co.uk
W: www.farmercopleys.co.uk

Farmer Copleys Farm Shop aims to produce home grown, animal friendly and local food.

Traditional butchery, fresh veg, local beers and British cheese and much more besides.

7 Keelham Hall Farm Shop

Victoria & James Robertshaw 01274 833472

Brighouse & Denholme Road, Thornton, Bradford, West Yorkshire BD13 3SS

F: 01274 833535
E: victoria@thefarmshop.net
W: www.keelhamhallfarmshop.co.uk

Keelham Hall Farm Shop offers a total "local" shopping experience. Our renowned in-house butchery department sells choice cuts of meat and meat-related products from prime quality stock - either reared on our own farm or sourced locally from Yorkshire farmers we know and trust.

We also have everything you can find in your local greengrocers, bakery, off-licence, delicatessen, garden centre or supermarket. Open 7 days a week.

Healthily

Organically

West Yorkshire

deliciouslyyorkshire

161

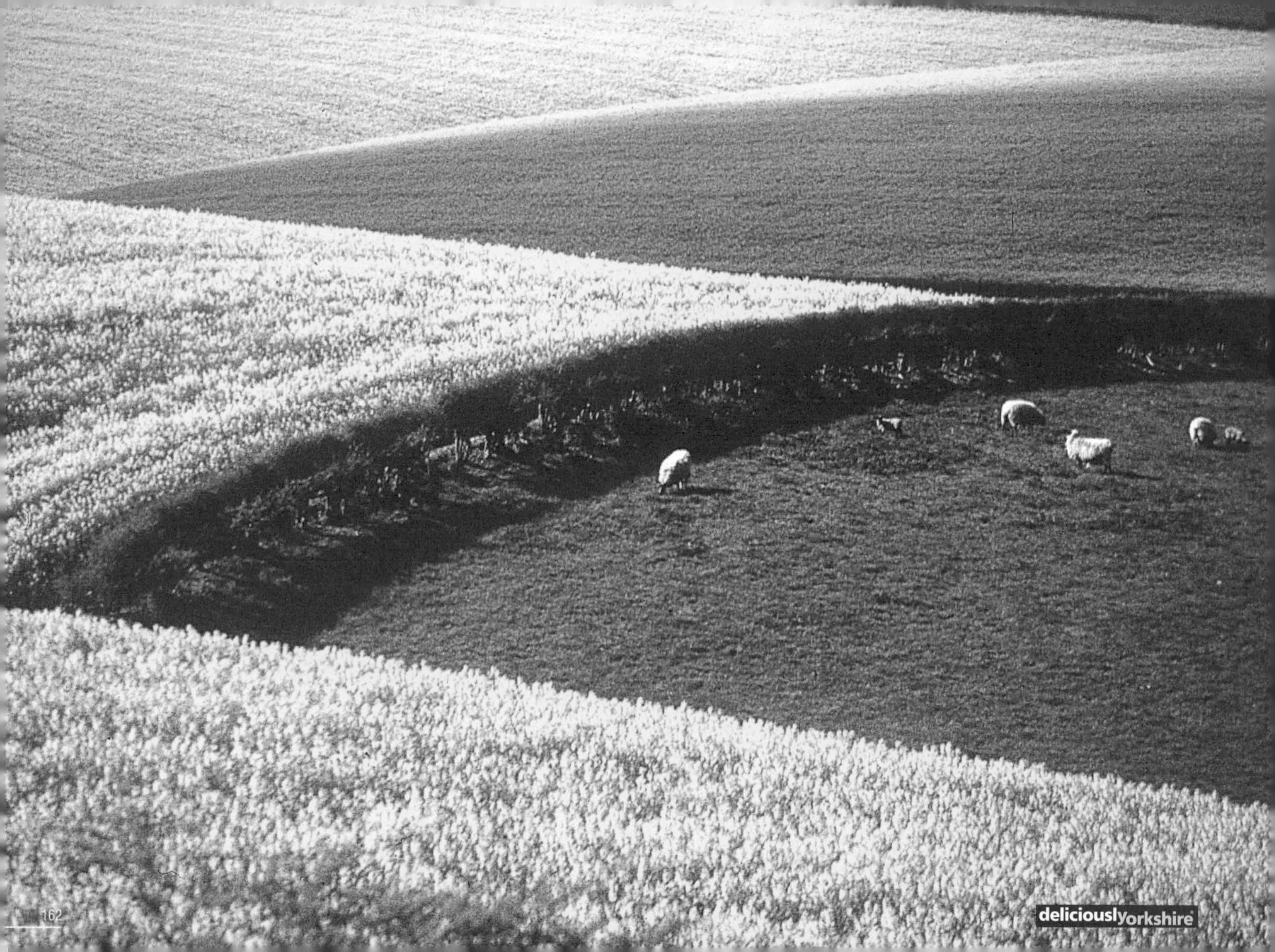

North/North East Lincolnshire

Adjoining North and North East Lincolnshire runs down to the Humber and boasts one of the country's largest and busiest fish docks.

This highly productive area produces some 20% of the UK's food and local specialities include Grimsby Haddock, Lincolnshire sausages, luxury hand-made crisps and award-winning pies stocked by the posh people's Knightsbridge grocer.

Huge expanses of its countryside and coast are still undeveloped and the Wolds are an area of outstanding natural beauty. Both attract wildlife and bird watchers, while the slower pace of life attracts golfers, walkers and cyclists alike. Deeply routed to the heritage of England, Lincolnshire retains many fine Georgian properties from the 19th century.

As well as the Deliciouslyorkshire brand, Lincolnshire producers who operate predominantly out of the Greater Lincolnshire area from the Humber to the Wash can also use the Select Lincolnshire and the Taste of Lincolnshire brands. Aiming to showcase the quality and range of local Lincolnshire produce and services in a market that grows progressively more crowded, you can find out more about Lincolnshire produce on either **www.selectlincolnshire.com** or **www.visitlincolnshire.com**.

North/North East Lincolnshire

North/North East Lincolnshire Food Highlights

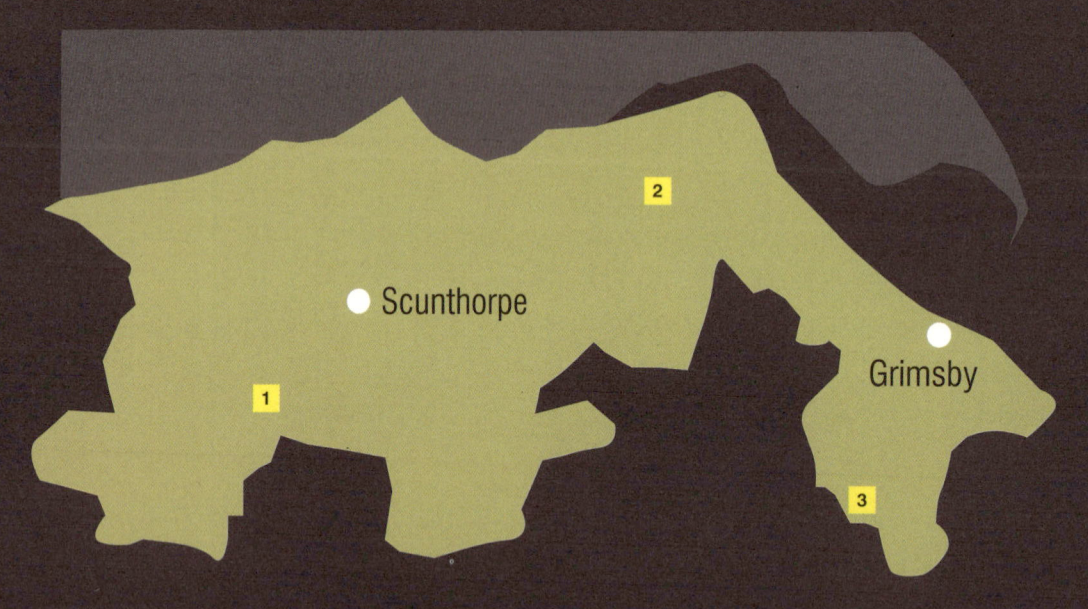

1 Redhill Farm Free Range Pork
Free range pork *(see entry on p165)*

2 Pipers Crisps
Crisp maker *(see entry on p165)*

3 Ideal Lincs Ltd
Wholesaler and distributor *(see entry on p165)*

Useful contacts
www.livelincolnshire.com
www.selectlincolnshire.com
www.deliciouslyyorkshire.co.uk

Producers

Meat, poultry and game – fresh and smoked

00 see food highlight map on page 164

Distributors

1 Redhill Farm Free Range Pork

Jane Tomlinson 01427 628 270

Blyton Carr, Gainsborough,
Lincolnshire DN21 3DT

E: jane@redhillfarm.com
W: www.redhillfarm.com

Redhill Farm are the real thing! Real farmers who produce everything by hand on their farm. Once tasted customers are converted - their pork is **slowly reared, succulent and full of flavour**. They are popularly known at Farmers Markets **as the stall with a queue!** See website for nearest Farmers Market.

Prepared food

2 Pipers Crisps

Alex Albone 01652 686 960

Wellington House, Wellington Way,
Elsham, Brigg, Lincolnshire DN20 0SP

F: 01652 686 965
E: alex@piperscrisps.com
W: www.piperscrisps.com

We are proud to use locally grown potatoes and natural flavours sourced from our friends who are passionate about quality, i.e. salt from Halen Mon on Anglesey, John Alvis's cheddar and cider vinegar from Julian Temperley.

We even have sweet chilli from The Genovese family in Bedfordshire.

3 Ideal Lincs Ltd

Paul Davey 01507 313 855

Grange Offices, Girsby Lane, Burgh on Baine,
Market Rasen, Lincolnshire LN8 6LA

F: 08703 835 280
E: paul@ideal-lincs.co.uk
W: www.ideal-lincs.co.uk

Specialist wholesaler & distributor of the finest fresh & ambient produce from the East Riding of Yorkshire & Humber region and Lincolnshire.

Supplying into multiple retailers and the national wholesale markets operating a regional produce hub for Asda, specailising in value added produce.

North/North East Lincolnshire

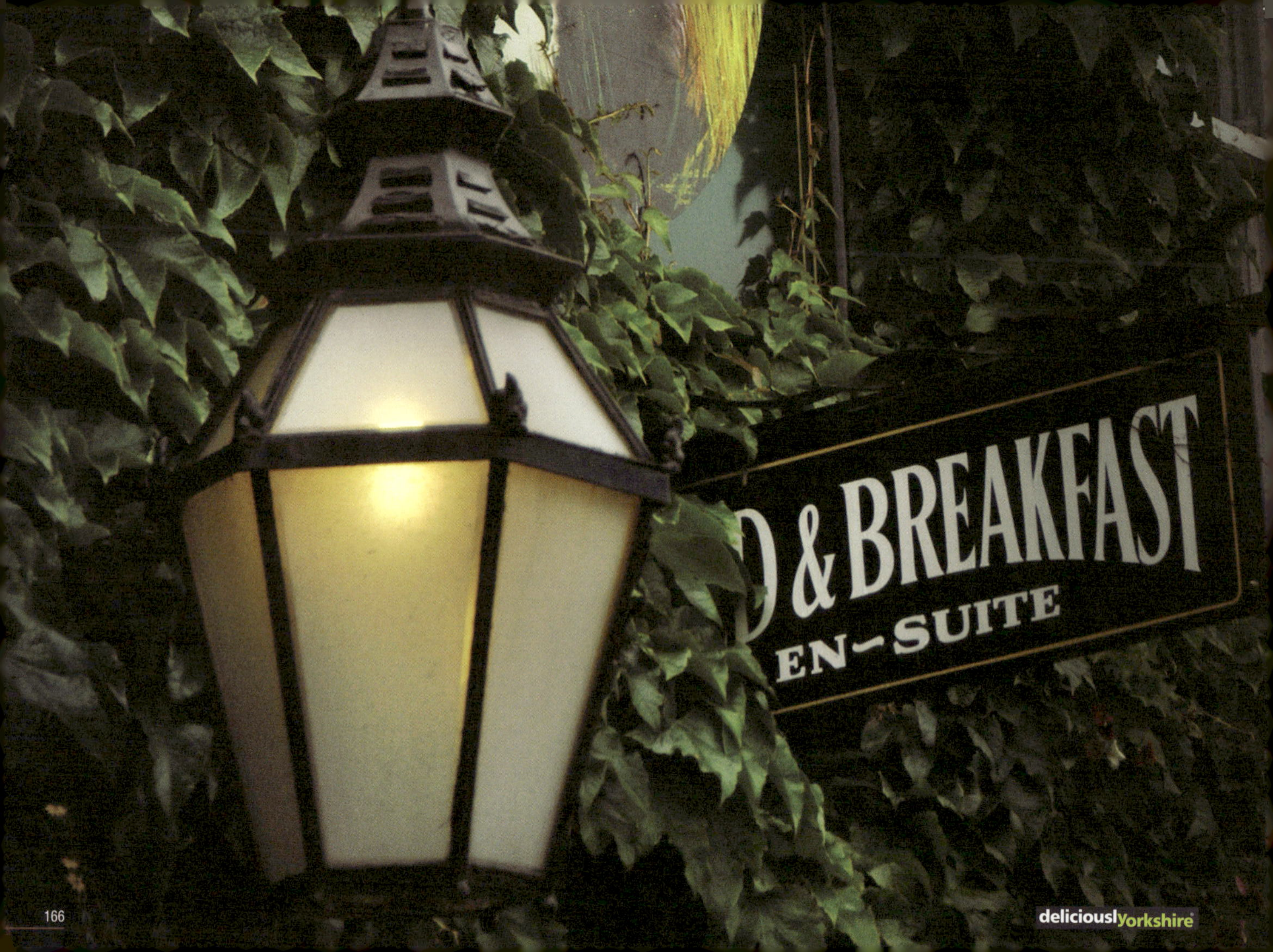
D & BREAKFAST
EN-SUITE

deliciouslyorkshire breakfast Members

A truly distinctive Yorkshire experience isn't complete without enjoying a lovingly-made breakfast from fresh, local ingredients.

The Deliciouslyorkshire Breakfast Scheme is run in association with the Yorkshire Tourist Board.

Extend your Yorkshire experience by taking a closer look at our excellent Deliciouslyorkshire Breakfast Members, all of whom are committed to including at least five locally sourced ingredients on their breakfast menus. Who can resist fresh, crusty bread, organic fruit-packed muesli, fat, juicy sausages, locally-cured bacon, Whitby-caught kippers or lightly scrambled eggs from the hens just outside your bedroom window? What a way to start the day!

To view online listings visit
www.deliciouslyorkshire.co.uk or
www.yorkshire.com

deliciously yorkshire
breakfast Members

North Yorkshire

17 Burgate

Pat Oxley   01751 473 463

17 Burgate, Pickering,
North Yorkshire YO18 7AU

- **F:** 01751 473 463
- **E:** info@17burgate.co.uk
- **W:** www.17burgate.co.uk

5 star gold award winning townhouse between castle and market place. Unashamed luxury for the weary traveller.

Log fire, secluded garden, internet access, special packages. Deliciouslyorkshire breakfast.

Apricot Lodge

Darran Bilton   01751 477 744

25 Crossgate Lane, Pickering,
North Yorkshire YO18 7EX

- **E:** apricotlodge@beeb.net
- **W:** www.apricotlodge.com

In a quiet spot overlooking fields within easy walking distance of Pickering. For our bedrooms and outstanding service we have been awarded the ETC 5 Star Rating. We serve delicious breakfasts of the highest standard using as much locally sourced ingredients as possible. You really can taste quality.

Ascot Lodge Guest House

Ken & Sandra Hudson   01904 798 234

112 Acomb Road, York,
North Yorkshire YO24 4EY

- **F:** 01904 786 742
- **E:** info@ascotlodge.com
- **W:** www.ascotlodge.com

Impressive Victorian house, beautifully refurbished offering high standards of comfort and cleanliness.
TV/ Video, hairdryer and hospitality trays. NON SMOKING THROUGHOUT. Convenient for attractions, coast and Dales. Free secure private parking.

Ashberry Hotel

Kevin Lyon   01904 647 339

103 The Mount, York,
North Yorkshire YO24 1AX

- **F:** 01904 647 339
- **E:** ashbury@talk21.com
- **W:** clients.thisisyork.co.uk/ashberry

The Ashberry is located in York. Charming Victorian house situated on The Mount, gateway to the city.

Five minutes walk to city walls, ten minutes to city centre, railway station, racecourse, minster and all other tourist attractions.

deliciouslyyorkshire
breakfast Members

North Yorkshire

Bank Villa

Liz Howard-Barker 01765 689 605

deliciouslyyorkshire breakfast | *Yorkshire Tourist Board Member* | *AA ★★★★ Guest House*

Masham, Ripon,
North Yorkshire HG4 4DB
- E: bankvilla@btopenworld.com
- W: www.bankvilla.com

Comfortable accommodation, award winning breakfast and dinner. Book a table in our licensed restaurant or visit our seasonal cafe.
Both offering home cooked local and home grown produce.

Barker Stakes Farm

Steven Goodfellow 01751 476 759

Lendales Lane, Pickering,
North Yorkshire YO18 8EE
- E: steve@barkerstakesfarm.com
- W: www.barkerstakesfarm.com

18th Century farmhouse B&B set in 32 acres, 1 mile from Pickering. After a peaceful nights sleep enjoy a breakfast of local produce in our conservatory.

Baytree House

Simon Picton 01423 564 493

98 Franklin Road, Harrogate,
North Yorkshire HG1 5EN
- F: 01423 563 554
- E: info@baytreeharrogate.co.uk
- W: www.baytreeharrogate.co.uk

Baytree House, Harrogate is ideally located right in the heart of North Yorkshire – perfect for those looking for a short stay. We're here to make your stay enjoyable and memorable.

Bootham Gardens Guesthouse

Ian Barnard 01904 625 911

47 Bootham Crescent, York,
North Yorkshire YO30 7AJ
- E: guesthouse@hotmail.co.uk
- W: www.bootham-gardens-guesthouse.co.uk

Purpose built luxury guesthouse, private parking, minutes walk to York Minster, a breakfast restaurant for residents serving the finest Yorkshire produce.

Brooklands Guest House

Carole Dean 01423 564 609

5 Valley Drive, Harrogate,
North Yorkshire HG2 0JJ
- E: brooklandsbb@supanet.com
- W: www.enjoyharrogate.com

Brooklands is a family run guesthouse.
Providing a Deliciouslyyorkshire breakfast with locally sourced produce. All four guestrooms are en-suite and include "Grandma Wilds Biscuits" and bottled Harrogate Spa Water.

deliciouslyyorkshire
breakfast Members

North Yorkshire

Broom House

Maria White 01947 895 279

Broom House Lane, Egton Bridge,
North Yorkshire YO21 1XD

F: 01947 895 657
E: mw@broom-house.co.uk
W: www.egton-bridge.co.uk

Offering 4-star silver accomodation in the picturesque village of Egton Bridge, this tranquil guest house sits on a hill with wonderful countryside views from every room.

Highly commended in the 2006 Discover Yorkshire Coast Tourism awards. Well-equipped, quality furnished en suite rooms are complemented by a traditional breakfast room and lounge. Enjoy fresh local produce in peaceful surroundings!

Clocktower at Rudding Park

01423 871 350

Follifoot, Harrogate,
North Yorkshire HG3 1JH

F: 01423 872 286
E: sales@ruddingpark.com
W: www.ruddingpark.com

Clocktower, Rudding Park's contemporary restaurant and bar features a cosmopolitan fusion of interior design inspirations from all over the world.

The menu celebrates the finest Yorkshire food using locally sourced ingredients. The Yorkshire tapas are a speciality and can be enjoyed with a drink, or just as a light snack!

Open all day, everyday.

Cedar Court (Harrogate)

Michael Weaver 01423 858 585

Park Parade, Harrogate,
North Yorkshire HG1 5AH

F: 01274 406 600
E: info@cedarcourthotels.co.uk
W: www.cedarcourthotels.co.uk

Cedar Court prides itself on sourcing local produce & food in our menus.

Our current group initative has been our successful Yorkshire Breakfast menu in all of our hotels.

Cundall Lodge Farm B&B

Caroline Barker 01423 360 203

Cundall Lodge Farm, Cundall,
York, North Yorkshire YO61 2RN

F: 01423 360 805
E: info@lodgefarmbb.co.uk
W: www.lodgefarmbb.co.uk

Farmhouse Breakfast Member

deliciously yorkshire
breakfast Members

North Yorkshire

Dean Court Hotel
David Brooks 01904 625 082

Duncombe Place, York,
North Yorkshire YO1 7EF
F: 01904 620 305
E: sales@deancourt-york.co.uk
W: www.deancourt-york.co.uk

The most important meal of the day- and one which elicits the most compliments. Waffles and Eggs benedict plus real porridge add to the strongly local- produce conventional dishes. There's a good vegetarian selection too. Stunning view of the Minster are reasons enough to make a beeline for breakfast at the Dean Court.

Dunsley Hall Country House Hotel
Bill Ward 01947 893 437

Dunsley, Whitby,
North Yorkshire YO21 3TL
F: 01947 893 505
E: reception@dunsleyhall.com
W: www.dunsleyhall.com

Dunsley Hall's award winning restaurant provides locally supplied ingredients and seafood is a speciality. Lunch time, early evening meals and snacks in the Pyman Bar provide a light alternative. Once home for a Victorian shipping magnate with 26 en-suite rooms, 18 individually furnished, some with 4 poster beds, and eight tastefully furnished new rooms recently added.

Gallon House
Rick & Sue Hodgson 01423 862 102

47 Kirkgate, Knaresborough,
North Yorkshire HG5 8BZ
E: gallon-house@ntlworld.com
W: www.gallon-house.co.uk

Situated overlooking Knaresborough's beautiful Nidd Gorge, Gallon House offers charming accommodation and delicious locally sourced food, prepared by well known Yorkshire Chef, Rick Hodgson. We, Rick and Sue, run the hotel personally, and take great pride in delivering an excellent standard of service and attention to detail in all things, the perfect antidote to a corporate hotel experience. A recent customer said 'Thank you for making your special place, our special place'.

North Yorkshire

breakfast Members

Elmfield House

Astra Towning 01677 450 558

Arrathorne, Bedale,
North Yorkshire DL8 1NE

E: stay@elmfieldhouse.co.uk
W: www.elmfieldhouse.co.uk

Award winning B&B using wholesome ingredients sourced mainly within 6 miles, including organic milk, cream and butter and our own free range eggs, locally smoked haddock, traditional sausages, local bacon and home made marmalades.

Grassington Lodge

Diane Lowe 01756 752 518

8 Wood Lane, Grassington,
North Yorkshire BD23 5LU

E: relax@grassingtonlodge.co.uk
W: www.grassingtonlodge.co.uk

Grassington Lodge is an award winning contemporary guest house, stylish and luxurious. Guests will experience first class hospitality and a friendly service. Quiet setting close to the centre of Grassington, the capital village of Upper Wharfedale.

Hotel du Vin

01423 856 800

Prospect Place, Harrogate,
North Yorkshire HG1 1LB

F: 01423 856 801
E: info@harrogate.hotelduvin.com
W: www.hotelduvin.com

Hotel du Vin and Bistro is a stylish hotel created from eight Georgian houses overlooking the stray. A different celebrated wine house sponsors each of the forty three stunning bedrooms. The Bistro offers classic dishes made with fresh ingredients which have been sourced from local suppliers and producers.

George and Dragon

01969 663 358

Aysgarth,
North Yorkshire DL8 3AD

F: 01969 663 773
E: info@georgeanddragonaysgarth.co.uk
W: www.georgeanddragonaysgarth.co.uk

Relax and indulge in privately owned 18th Century Hotel. Luxury en-suite bedrooms, excellent food, extensive wine list. Surprised, you will be!

Grimston House

Pat Wright 01904 728 328

Deighton, York,
North Yorkshire YO19 6HB

E: pat_wright@btinternet.com
W: www.grimstonhouse.com

Four star friendly guest house set in village location five miles from York on the bus route. Serves a delicious Yorkshire breakfast. Two minutes from local pub which serves wonderful home cooked food.

breakfast Members

Inglenook Guest House

Phil Smith   01524 241 270

20 Main Street, Ingleton,
North Yorkshire LA6 3HJ

E: inglenook20@hotmail.com
W: www.inglenookguesthouse.com

Yorkshire Dales – Ingleton. Quality B&B in delightful setting with superb views. Craven Accommodation Provider of the Year runner up. Hearty breakfasts. En-suite bedrooms. No smoking. AA/VB 4 stars.

King's Square Café

Angela Hawes   01904 631 662

28 Colliergate, York,
North Yorkshire YO1 8BN

E: hawes_276@fsmail.net

A traditional café in the centre of York serving freshly prepared and cooked local produce. Dishes range from full English breakfast to delicious home made soups, quiches and traditional home made cakes. Open daily for breakfast, lunch and afternoon teas.

Lockwoods

Matthew Lockwood   01765 607 555

83 North Street, Ripon,
North Yorkshire HG4 1DP

F: 01765 607 555
E: info@lockwoodsrestaurant.co.uk
W: www.lockwoodsrestaurants.co.uk

Lockwoods Cafébar/Restaurant aims to celebrate the best of Ripon's rich Cathedral City history, whilst challenging it into the future.

This theme of traditional and contemporary is reflected in our décor, our Modern European menu, our wine list, and the art on our walls. We use fresh and seasonal ingredients from local producers, and look forward to welcoming you!

Lovesome Hill Farm

Mrs Pearson   01609 772 311

Lovesome Hill, Northallerton,
North Yorkshire DL6 2PB

F: 01609 774 715
E: pearsonlhf@care4free.net
W: www.lovesomehill.co.uk

Sample our farmhouse breakfast using our own bacon and sausages when available and homemade preserves, local organic milk & butter. Help us to collect fresh free range eggs. There are also packs of our own lamb, pork and beef available to take home.

Low Penhowe

Philippa & Christopher Turner   01653 658 336

Burythorpe, Malton,
North Yorkshire YO17 9LU

F: 01653 658 619
E: lowpenhowe@btinternet.com
W: www.bedandbreakfastyorkshire.co.uk

A traditional Yorkshire stone-built farmhouse, with stunning views overlooking the Howardian Hills, Castle Howard & North Yorkshire Moors, the house makes an idyllic spot for a quiet few nights away yet close enough to York.
2006 Deliciouslyorkshire Best Yorkshire Breakfast Winner.

North Yorkshire

breakfast Members

North Yorkshire

Mill Close Farm

Patricia Knox 01677 450 257

Mill Close Farm, Patrick Brompton,
Bedale, North Yorkshire DL8 1JY
- **F:** 01748 813 612
- **E:** pat@millclose.co.uk
- **W:** www.millclose.co.uk

5 Star B&B with prestigious gold award in peaceful rural situation between the Yorkshire Dales and Yorkshire Moors. Luxurious ensuite rooms, 2 with spa baths. One 4 poster suite. Traditional and speciality breakfasts prepared with local produce.

New Inn Hotel

Keith Mannion 01524 251 203

Clapham, Nr Settle,
North Yorkshire LA2 8HH
- **E:** info@newinn-clapham.co.uk
- **W:** www.newinn-clapham.co.uk

Set in beautiful Yorkshire Dales providing accommodation for the traveller since 1776. Lovingly and carefully refurbished. You will experience a warm and friendly welcome.

Peasholm Park Hotel

Jeanette Frank 01723 500 954

21-23 Victoria Park, Scarborough,
North Yorkshire YO12 7TS
- **E:** peasholmparkhotel@btconnect.com
- **W:** www.peasholmpark.co.uk

Family owned & run guest accommodation, with a warm Yorkshire welcome.

12 bedrooms - all ensuite on 1st & 2nd floors. Close to bowling club, cricket club, Peasholm Park, beach & town centre.

Short distance from north & south cliff golf clubs, Stephen Joseph theatre & spa. Vegetarians also catered for with locally sourced breakfast produce.

Newton House

Lisa Wilson 01423 863 539

5-7 York Place, Knaresborough,
North Yorkshire HG5 0AD
- **E:** info@newtonhousehotel.com
- **W:** www.newtonhousehotel.com

Winner of multiple awards, many at national level. Newton House stunning luxurious and spacious en-suite accommodation with AA award winning breakfasts freshly cooked from an impressive menu. A highly recommended place to stay.

Phoenix Court

Alison & Bryan Edwards 01723 501 150

8/9 Rutland Terrace, Queens Parade,
Scarborough, North Yorkshire YO12 7JB
- **E:** info@hotel-phoenix.co.uk
- **W:** www.hotel-phoenix.co.uk

Phoenix Court offers excellent accommodation overlooking Scarborough's North Bay. Comfortable en-suite rooms, guest car park, bar, lounge and excellent food, topped off with friendly service and a smile.

deliciouslyyorkshire
breakfast Members

North Yorkshire

Rawcliffe House Farm

Jan & Duncan Allsopp   01751 473 292

Stape, Pickering,
North Yorkshire YO18 8JA

E: stay@rawcliffehousefarm.co.uk
W: www.rawcliffehousefarm.co.uk

We have three bedrooms situated on our south facing courtyard. We are proud to have been awarded a Silver Award for Excellence from the English Tourism Council. Every morning we serve a delicious full Yorkshire Breakfast using only the finest local produce.

Smugglers Rock Country House

Mrs S Gregson   01723 870 044

Staintandale, Ravenscar,
Scarborough, North Yorkshire YO13 0ER

E: info@smugglersrock.co.uk
W: www.smugglersrock.co.uk

Georgian country house, reputedly a former smugglers haunt between Whitby and Scarborough. Panoramic views over surrounding National Park and sea. An ideal holiday base for exploring the area, close to 'Heartbeat' country.

Strawberry House

Kamal Blanshard   01423 714 816

Street Lane, Bewerley, Nr Pateley Bridge,
North Yorkshire HG3 5JE

E: kamalblanshard@hotmail.com
W: www.strawberryhousebedandbreakfast.co.uk

Strawberry House offers a stunning location with views of Nidderdale in all directions. Luxury accomodation and a hearty locally sourced breakfast results in 4 star, silver award service for visitors.

Red Lea Hotel

01723 362 431

Prince of Wales Terrace, Scarborough,
North Yorkshire YO11 2AJ

E: info@redleahotel.co.uk
W: www.redleahotel.co.uk

Superbly located on Scarborough's south cliff and close to the Spa Cliff lift, the Red Lea enjoys lovely sea views.

With comfortable bedrooms, pleasant lounges, indoor swimming pool and great food, the hotel offers guest a warm welcome all year round.

Stoney End Holidays

Pamela Hague   01969 650 652

Stoney End, Worton, Leyburn,
North Yorkshire DL8 3ET

E: pmh@stoneyend.co.uk
W: www.stoneyend.co.uk

Stoney End is a B&B in the heart of the Yorkshire Dales.

We are passionate about food and our extensive breakfast menu is bursting with locally produced goodies.

Swinton Park

01765 680 900

Masham, Ripon,
North Yorkshire HG4 4JH

E: enquiries@swintonpark.com
W: www.swintonpark.com

Luxury castle hotel serving award winning cuisine with particular focus on ingredients sourced from the hotel's four acre walled garden. 30 bedrooms with spa, cookery school run by celebrity chef Rosemary Shrager, and country pursuits including golf, fishing and falconry.

deliciouslyyorkshire breakfast **Members**

North Yorkshire

The Almar

Beverley Rendell   01723 372 887

116 Columbus Ravine, Scarborough,
North Yorkshire YO12 7QZ

- **E:** bevandphill@rendellp.fsnet.co.uk
- **W:** www.thealmar.co.uk

Our North Bay hotel offers you quality bed and breakfast accommodation. A gold award smoke free environment and our Deliciouslyyorkshire Breakfast makes us a popular choice with guests.

The Carlton Lodge

Chris Parkin   01439 770 557

Bondgate, Helmsley, York,
North Yorkshire YO62 5EY

- **F:** 01439 770 623
- **E:** enquiries@carlton-lodge.com
- **W:** www.carlton-lodge.com

Our bed and breakfast accommodation comprises of just 8 cosy en suite rooms, two twins, 5 doubles and a single. All are individually furnished with local pine and include TV, DVD/CD player, radio, telephone, clock, tea and coffee tray. If you are looking to de-stress and relax we can make your stay memorable.

The Devonshire Fell Hotel & Restaurant

Andrew Forbes   01756 729 000

Burnsall, Nr Skipton,
North Yorkshire BD23 6BT

- **F:** 01756 729 009
- **E:** res@devonshirehotels.co.uk
- **W:** www.devonshirehotels.co.uk

City chic in the countryside with stunning views over Wharfedale - restaurant, bar, private events and 12 designer bedrooms. Serves scrummy food 7 days using fresh kitchen garden, estate produce & local suppliers.

The Boars Head Hotel & Ripley Castle

Steve Chesnutt   01423 771 888

The Boars Head Hotel, Ripley,
North Yorkshire HG3 3AY

- **F:** 01423 771 589
- **E:** reservations@boarsheadripley.co.uk
- **W:** www.boarsheadripley.co.uk

The Boars Head is a 25 bedroom luxury country house hotel, with a 2 Rosette fine dining room and a busy bar Bistro.

The Devonshire Arms Country House Hotel & Spa

Jane Scott   01756 710 441

Bolton Abbey, Skipton,
North Yorkshire BD23 6AJ

- **F:** 01756 710 564
- **E:** res@devonshirehotels.co.uk
- **W:** www.devonshirehotels.co.uk

Gracious unstuffy country estate hotel with two restaurants (Michelin star fine dining & vibrant bar brasserie), private dining, bedrooms & health spa. Delicious tasty food served using the best of extensive kitchen gardens, local landscape and seascape.

The Gallery

Kathryn Collington   01845 523 767

18 Kirkgate, Thirsk,
North Yorkshire YO7 1PQ

- **E:** kathryn@gallerybedandbreakfast.co.uk
- **W:** www.gallerybedandbreakfast.co.uk

Family run 4 Star B&B in a charming Grade II listed building. Three modern en-suite rooms and Deliciouslyyorkshire approved breakfasts.

Ideally located opposite James Herriot Centre and 100 yards from historic Thirsk market square.

breakfast Members

00 see food highlight map on page 54

The Golden Fleece

Jo Grewcock 01845 523 108

Market Place, Thirsk,
North Yorkshire YO7 1LL

- F: 01845 523 996
- E: reservations@goldenfleecehotel.com
- W: www.goldenfleecehotel.com

Lovely old coaching inn serving wonderful Yorkshire breakfast and traditional food. Excellent Sunday lunch, great value at £12.95 p p. 23 bedrooms all ensuite, a great venue for touring the Moors and Dales.

The Grange Hotel

Amie Postings 01904 644 744

1 Clifton, York,
North Yorkshire YO30 6AA

- F: 01904 612 453
- E: info@grangehotel.co.uk
- W: www.grangehotel.co.uk

A traditional Yorkshire breakfast in a traditional Yorkshire setting. Our Ivy Brasserie serves breakfast in the luxury surroundings of a typical Yorkshire grade two listed York house.

27 The Harmony Guest House

Nanette Evans 01723 373 562

13 Princess Royal Terrace, South Cliff,
Scarborough, North Yorkshire YO11 2RP

- E: harmonyguesthouse@hotmail.com
- W: www.theharmonyguesthouse.co.uk

We are a fun, famliy, veggie and dog friendly guest house. Informal atmosphere with great home cooking guaranteed. 100% non smoking, regionally sourced food.

Open all year. Weekend packages available. Five minute walk from the sea front.

The Kimberley Hotel

Rob Garrett 01423 505 613

11-19 Kings Road, Harrogate,
North Yorkshire HG1 5JY

- F: 01423 530 276
- E: rob@thekimberley.co.uk
- W: www.thekimberley.co.uk

Enjoy the best breakfast in Harrogate. You can sample local pork sausages, Yorkshire dry cured bacon, freshly baked bloomer bread and over 14 varieties of locally made jams, marmalade and chutney and much more…

The Kings Head Hotel and Restaurant

Reception 01642 722 318

The Green, Newton-under-Roseberry,
Nr Great Ayton, North Yorkshire TS9 6QR

- F: 01642 724 750
- E: info@kingsheadhotel.co.uk
- W: www.kingsheadhotel.co.uk

A delightful family owned hotel & restaurant sited at the foot of Roseberry Topping - on the edge of the North York Moors National Park. Serving lunch and evening meals using high quality produce sourced from the local area.

North Yorkshire

deliciouslyyorkshire
breakfast **Members**

North Yorkshire

00 see food highlight map on page 54

The Lodge at Leeming Bar
Leslie Clarke 01677 422 122

The Great North Road, Leeming Bar,
Bedale, North Yorkshire DL8 1DT
- **F:** 01677 424 507
- **E:** thelodgeatleemingbar@btconnect.com
- **W:** www.leemingbar.com

The Lodge is conveniently located just off the A1 at Bedale. The comfortable 39 roomed Lodge with shop, restaurant, café, bar and meeting rooms is ideal for the business and leisure traveller.

The Old Town Hall Guest House & Tea Room
Julie & Simon Greenslade 01969 625 641

The Old Town Hall, Redmire,
Leyburn, North Yorkshire DL8 4ED
- **F:** 01969 624 982
- **E:** tea@theoldtownhall.co.uk
- **W:** www.theoldtownhall.co.uk

Luxury family run guest house and tea room in the heart of Wensleydale offering superb food using locally produced ingredients, served in a welcoming homely Yorkshire setting. Closed Wednesdays.

30 The Plough Inn At Wigglesworth
Steve Amplett 01729 840 243

Wigglesworth, Skipton,
North Yorkshire BD23 4RJ
- **F:** 01729 840 401
- **E:** sue@ploughinn.info
- **W:** www.ploughinn.info

The 18C Plough Inn is beautifully positioned between the Yorkshire Dales and Forest of Bowland. Our menus feature many locally sourced products - lamb, beef, pork are bought from farms within three miles of the Inn. We have 9 en-suite bedrooms and a conservatory restaurant with fantastic views over the Dales.

The White Swan Inn
Lisa Fraser 01751 472 288

Market Place, Pickering,
North Yorkshire YO18 7AA
- **F:** 01751 475 554
- **E:** welcome@white-swan.co.uk
- **W:** www.white-swan.co.uk

You will discover we have a clear ethos. Simple goodness from fresh ingredients that are sourced in season, properly cooked, presented and put on your table with a minimum of food miles. You will be eating at the only restaurant outside of London supplied by the famous 'Ginger Pig' farm/butchery.

178

deliciously yorkshire
breakfast Members

The Poplars
Mrs Chilton   01845 522 712

Carlton Miniott, Thirsk,
North Yorkshire YO7 4LX
- F: 01845 522 712
- E: info@poplars-cottages.co.uk
- W: www.poplars-cottages.co.uk

A warm welcome awaits you in our friendly home. Beautiful en-suite rooms, enjoy a delicious breakfast with lots of choice. After a lovely day out relax in the garden or sitting room with tea and cakes.

Well House
Judith Smith   01609 772 253

Newby Wiske, Northallerton,
North Yorkshire DL7 9EX
- F: 01609 772 253

Well House is a beautiful Georgian House set in the picturesque conservation village of Newby Wiske.

There is a choice of breakfasts, freshly prepared with all local ingredients.

The Grand St Ledger Hotel
01302 364 111

Bennetthorpe, Doncaster,
South Yorkshire DN2 6AX
- F: 01302 329 865
- E: sales@grandstleger.com
- W: www.grandstleger.com

Set opposite Doncaster Racecourse and just outside the bustling Doncaster Town Centre, the 3 Star Grand St. Leger Hotel offers the finest accommodation in Doncaster and is a great base to explore Doncaster, Yorkshire and the rest of Northern England.

Watermill House B&B
Lionel & Alison Barnes   01677 423 240

Watermill House, Little Crakehall,
Bedale, North Yorkshire DL8 1HU
- E: stay@crakehallwatermill.co.uk
- W: www.crakehallwatermill.co.uk

Watermill House is a bed and breakfast establishment located near Bedale. It offers a warm welcome and personal attention to detail. Come and enjoy the beauty of North Yorkshire, whatever the season and relax.

Wynnstay House
Andy and Tracey Davis   01423 560 476

60 Franklin Road, Harrogate,
North Yorkshire HG1 5EE
- E: wynnstayhouse@tiscali.co.uk
- W: www.wynnstayhouse.com

4 Star guest house & self catering cottage in the centre of Harrogate. Stylishly decorated rooms extensive breakfast menu offering fresh local produce.
Visit www.wynnstayhouse.com

Lovingly Made

deliciously yorkshire

North Yorkshire/South Yorkshire

deliciously yorkshire
breakfast Members

High Catton Grange - B&B & Self Catering

Sheila Foster   01759 371 374

High Catton Grange, Stamford Bridge,
York, East Yorkshire YO41 1EP

F: 01759 371 374
E: enquire@highcattongrange.co.uk
W: www.highcattongrange.co.uk

Delightful 18th century farmhouse B&B. A warm welcome awaits you.

En-suite & private facilities, peaceful rural location near York. Deliciouslyorkshire Breakfast served.

Little Weghill Farm

Jennifer Dimishky   01482 897 650

Weghill Road, Preston,
East Yorkshire HU12 8SX

F: 01482 897 650
E: info@littleweghillfarm.co.uk
W: www.littleweghillfarm.co.uk

Enjoy a traditional English breakfast. We use locally produced dry cured bacon and sausages, free range eggs, Hull smoked kippers, and honey and marmalade made in the next village.

Rags Hotel Bar and Restaurant

Julie Dyl   01262 400 355

Rags

South Pier, Bridlington,
East Yorkshire YO15 3AN

F: 01262 674 729
E: ragshotel@tesco.net
W: www.ragshotel.co.uk

A restaurant with Rooms, Rags has contemporary styled en-suite bedrooms some with spectacular views. Full Yorkshire breakfast is served in the harbour view restaurant. Our modern bar and harbour view sun lounge serves our full menu every day with locally sourced produce such as freshly caught Sea Bass and Bridlington Crab.

Call in for a meal, snack or coffee any time and watch the bustling life of the harbour from our spectacular views.

42 The Calls

Nigel Stanley   01132 440 099

42 The Calls, Leeds,
West Yorkshire LS2 7EW

F: 01132 440 099
E: hotel@42thecalls.co.uk
W: www.42thecalls.co.uk

This refreshingly different, townhouse hotel, has a unique location, with the advantage of a peaceful setting overlooking the River Aire and being only a few minutes walk from the city centre. 42 The Calls, was converted in 1991 from a cornmill and since opening, has won no fewer than 10 major awards or accolades.

Ashmount Guest House

Gill Crennell   01535 645 726

Mytholmes Lane, Haworth,
West Yorkshire BD22 8EZ

E: enquiries@ashmounthaworth.co.uk
W: www.ashmounthaworth.co.uk

Stay in the former home of Dr. Amos Ingham, physician to Charlotte and Patrick Bronte. Built in 1870 the original Gothic interiors of the house are well preserved and most of the furnishings are Victorian. Fantastic views of the moors.

deliciously yorkshire
breakfast Members

West Yorkshire

Cedar Court (Bradford)
Michael Weaver 01274 406 606

Mayo Avenue, Off Rooley Lane,
Bradford, West Yorkshire BD5 8HZ
- **F:** 01274 406 600
- **E:** sales@cedarcourtbradford.co.uk
- **W:** www.cedarcourthotels.co.uk

Cedar Court prides itself on sourcing local produce & food in our menus.

Our current group initative has been our successful Yorkshire Breakfast menu in all of our hotels.

Cedar Court (Wakefield)
Michael Weaver 01924 276 310

Calder Grove, Denby Dale Road,
Wakefield, West Yorkshire WF4 3QZ
- **E:** info@cedarcourthotels.co.uk
- **W:** www.cedarcourthotels.co.uk

Cedar Court prides itself on sourcing local produce & food in our menus.

Our current group initative has been our successful Yorkshire Breakfast menu in all of our hotels.

Field House B&B
Pat Horrocks-Taylor 01422 355 457

Staups Lane, Stump Cross,
Halifax, West Yorkshire HX3 6XW
- **E:** stayatfieldhouse@yahoo.co.uk
- **W:** www.fieldhouse-bb.co.uk

Offering guests a warm and friendly welcome, this Grade II listed Yorkshire B&B near Halifax/Shibden Hall offers a lounge with open fire and is set in countryside, Field House Bed and Breakfast is an exquisite Grade II listed building full of charm and character, and beautifully appointed.

Cedar Court (Huddersfield)
Michael Weaver 01422 375 431

Ainley Top, Huddersfield,
West Yorkshire HD3 3RH
- **F:** 01422 314 050
- **E:** info@cedarcourthotels.co.uk
- **W:** www.cedarcourthotels.co.uk

Cedar Court prides itself on sourcing local produce & food in our menus.

Our current group initative has been our successful Yorkshire Breakfast menu in all of our hotels.

Dimple Well Lodge
Susan & Enzo Sechi 01924 264 352

35 The Green, Ossett,
West Yorkshire WF5 8JX
- **F:** 01924 274 024
- **E:** thedimplewell@btconnect.com
- **W:** www.dimple-well-lodge-hotel.co.uk

Set in an acre of beautiful grounds, this delightful family run hotel, provides an ideal venue for business and pleasure.

Four Gables
Anne & David Watts 01937 845 592

Oaks Lane, Boston Spa,
West Yorkshire LS23 6DS
- **E:** info@fourgables.co.uk
- **W:** www.fourgables.co.uk

Four Gables is a charming Arts & Crafts home with a wealth of period features, serving as a B&B with a five diamond rating. David and Anne pride themselves on their attention to detail which applies to the rooms as much as their generous Yorkshire breakfast featuring local produce, homemade jams etc.

West Yorkshire

breakfast Members

00 see food highlight map on page 140

---

2 Holdsworth House

Sophia Williams 01422 240 024

HOLDSWORTH HOUSE
HOTEL & RESTAURANT

Holdsworth, Halifax,
West Yorkshire HX2 9TG

F: 01422 244 101
E: sophia@holdsworthhouse.co.uk
W: www.holdsworthhouse.co.uk

A listed Jacobean house located in the heart of Pennine Yorkshire, Holdsworth House boasts forty bedrooms and suites, a stunning restaurant serving exquisite local food, roaring fires, a glorious parterre garden and a reputation for stylish service.

Family owned since 1963 the hotel is just 7 miles from the M62 and provides the ideal setting for celebrations of every kind.

Holme House

01422 847 588

HOLME HOUSE

enjoyEngland.com Silver Award

enjoyEngland.com Bed & Breakfast

New Road, Hebden Bridge,
West Yorkshire HX7 8AD

F: 01422 847 354
E: mail@holmehousehebdenbridge.co.uk
W: www.holmehousehebdenbridge.co.uk

A charming Georgian house situated in the centre of Hebden Bridge, Holme House offers five star rated accommodation and a delicious breakfast menu.

All rooms are furnished to a high standard having TV, DVD, hospitality tray and complementary toiletries. Price from £35 per person per night.

Malmaison

01133 981 000

Malmaison LEEDS

1 Swinegate, Leeds,
West Yorkshire LS1 4AG

F: 01133 981 002
E: leeds@malmaison.com
W: www.malmaison.com

Malmaison is a design-led hotel, full of character and located in the city centre.

The bar and brasserie are the heart and soul of the hotel. We work with local producers and suppliers to offer our 'home grown and local' menu - all dishes include fresh, organic ingredients.

---

deliciouslyyorkshire

deliciouslyyorkshire
breakfast Members

West Yorkshire

Manor Guest House
Michele or Michael Carter   01535 274 374

The Manor, Sutton Drive, Cullingworth,
Bradford, West Yorkshire BD13 5BQ
- **F:** 01535 274 374
- **E:** info@cullingworthmanor.co.uk
- **W:** www.cullingworthmanor.co.uk

Lovingly restored this 18th Century Manor House is enhanced by many original features. Ideally situated for exploring the rugged Pennine Moorland of Bronte country, the Yorkshire Dales and beyond.

Radisson SAS
Tom Gibson   01132 366 000

No.1 The Light, The Headrow,
Leeds, West Yorkshire LS1 8TL
- **E:** info.leeds@radissonsas.com
- **W:** www.leeds.radissonsas.com

Radisson SAS Hotel Leeds with convenient facilities and extensive conferencing and meeting venues, is the ideal destination for business or leisure travellers alike.

Rombalds Hotel & Restaurant
Colin Clarkson   01943 603 201

Best Western
ROMBALDS HOTEL & RESTAURANT

West View, Wells Road,
Ilkley, West Yorkshire LS29 9JG
- **F:** 01943 816 586
- **E:** colinclarkson@rombaldshotel.fsnet.co.uk
- **W:** www.rombalds.co.uk

Rombalds, 'Ilkley's premier hotel' is set in a Georgian terrace on the edge of Ilkley Moor yet only 600 yards from the beautiful town centre.

The hotel boasts a 2 AA rosetted restaurant and in 2007 was winner of the sought after Best Western North Eastern Hotel of the Year.

Pickersgill Manor Farm B&B
Lisa Preston   01535 655 228

Low Lane, Silsden,
West Yorkshire BD20 9JH
- **E:** info@dalesfarmhouse.co.uk
- **W:** www.dalesfarmhouse.co.uk

Pickersgill Manor Farm is a working farm situated on Silsden Moor. We are a modern farmhouse with a traditional feel, and have created the perfect place to get away.

Thirstily

deliciouslyyorkshire

183

deliciousyorkshire breakfast Members

West Yorkshire

00 see food highlight map on page 140

Rosebud Cottage Guest House

Caroline Starkey   01535 640 321

1 Belle Isle Road, Haworth,
Keighley, West Yorkshire BD22 8OQ

- **F:** 01535 646 720
- **E:** info@rosebudcottage.co.uk
- **W:** www.rosebudcottage.co.uk

Rosebud Cottage is a typical stone built Yorkshire cottage dating back to 1752 with fine features and character offering traditional Yorkshire breakfasts.

Evening meals can also be pre-booked and enjoyed in our cosy dining room overlooking the garden, all our ingredients are of a high quality and locally sourced.

Sunnybank

Peter White   01484 684 857

78 Upperthong Lane, Holmfirth,
West Yorkshire HD9 3BQ

- **E:** info@sunnybankguesthouse.co.uk
- **W:** www.sunnybankguesthouse.co.uk

Sunny Bank is relaxed, comfortable and combines luxury accomodation with fantastic service and attention to detail. Surrounded by 2 acres of mature wooded gardens and with spacious car parking we have three en-suite bedrooms all elegantly finished.

The Dusty Miller

Phillip Webster   01422 885 959

Burnley Road, Mytholmroyd,
Hebden Bridge, West Yorkshire HX7 5LH

- **F:** 01422 885 959
- **E:** thedustymiller@hotmail.com
- **W:** www.dustymiller.co.uk

The Dusty Miller is a Grade II listed building dating back to the 18th Century, situated in the picturesque village of Mytholmroyd nestled in the Calder Valley. The property had run into dis-repair over a number of years, and the present refurbishment of £750,000 will bring this prominent building back to its former glory.

3 The Old Registry

Paul Widdowson   01535 646 503

2-4 Main Street, Haworth,
West Yorkshire BD22 8DA

- **F:** 01535 646 503
- **E:** enquiries@theoldregistryhaworth.co.uk
- **W:** www.theoldregistryhaworth.co.uk

A luxurious resting place in the heart of Brontë country. Dedicated to the Deliciousyorkshire campaign our breakfast suppliers include Arthur Haigh, Bleikers, Farmhouse Preserves and we work very closely with Lishman's of Ilkley who produce our bacon and make our sauages by request, without any preservatives, stabilisers, colourants etc.

deliciously yorkshire
breakfast Members

00 see food highlight map on page 140

West Yorkshire

The Huddersfield Central Lodge

Joe Marsden or Angela Hincliffe 01484 515 551

11-15 Beast Market, Huddersfield,
West Yorkshire HD1 1QF

F: 01484 432 349
E: enquiries@centrallodge.com
W: www.centrallodge.com

Rooms are all en-suite and are available in family size, double, twin and single. Rates are at sensible prices and include continental style breakfast, and or full English Breakfast.

Tower House Executive Guest House

Carol Scatter 01977 699 988

21 Bondgate, Pontefract,
West Yorkshire WF8 2JP

F: 01977 707 111
E: towerhouse.guesthouse@virgin.net
W: www.towerhouseguesthouse.com

Rich in history & comfort. A stunning Victorian house restored to it's original elegance and offering elegantly decorated bedrooms and extensive hotel facilities having just been awarded the highest standards in tourism.

---

5   Watermill Restaurant (Milford Hotel)

Shaun Sleath 01977 681 800

Watermill
Restaurant & Private Dining Rooms

Great North Road, Peckfield,
Leeds, West Yorkshire LS25 5LQ

F: 01977 681 245
E: enquiries@mlh.co.uk
W: www.mlh.co.uk

Treat yourself to one of our fine Yorkshire breakfasts including award winning sausages with dry cured bacon, free range eggs and locally grown field mushrooms; all followed by wholemeal toast with Yorkshire heather honey or local jams and marmalades. Locally smoked kippers & haddock also available. Traditional Sunday lunch served 12 noon to 9pm. Yorkshire reared sirloin of beef always featured. Evening menu served 6pm to 10pm Monday to Saturday & changing constantly to reflect availability of local produce. Three private dining rooms available.

The Railway Hotel

John Chew 01422 351 209

29 Horton Street, Halifax,
West Yorkshire HX1 1QE

F: 01422 351 209
W: www.railwayhotelhalifax.co.uk

Characterful 10 bedroom traditional Inn next to Halifax's historic Piece Hall, with parking, in house produced breakfasts, bar meals & sandwiches. Locally brewed real ale, parties catered for.

Creatively Plated

---

deliciously yorkshire

185

Specialist Services to the Food Industry

Specialist Services to the Food Industry

a really cool company

David Copley 07739 467 360

39 Harewood Mews, Harewood,
Leeds, West Yorkshire LS17 9LY

E: info@davidcopley.com
W: www.areallycoolcompany.co.uk

a really cool company specialises in the bespoke delivery of temperature controlled food and pharmaceutical samples throughout the UK and Europe. Occasional deliveries and distribution, but London weekly!

Andrew M Jackson

Hugh Smith 01482 325 242

Essex House, Manor Street,
Hull, East Yorkshire HU1 1XH

F: 01482 212 974
E: hes@amj.co.uk
W: www.amj.co.uk

Business Lawyers. For your every need in forming, running, maintaining and protecting your business and personal interests. Small business or large – we can help.

Bow House Limited

Richard Fox 01347 821 928

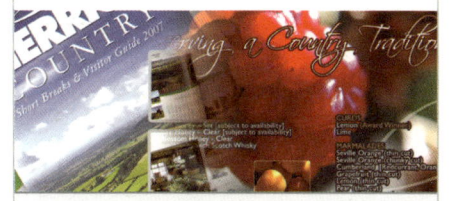

116 Long Street, Easingwold,
York, North Yorkshire YO61 3JA

F: 01347 822 943
E: richard@bowhouse.co.uk
W: www.bowhouse.co.uk

Bursting with fresh ideas, Bow House's talented and versitile team offers a blend of expertise and creative flair in design.

Whether you're looking for branding, websites or print (including publications, packaging, advertising and marketing materials), please get in touch to see what we have to offer (or view our portfolio online).

Abacus 155 Ltd

Stuart Baldwin 08700 502 212

4 Spring Bank Meadow, Ripon,
North Yorkshire HG4 1HQ

E: stuart.baldwin@abacusnetwork.co.uk
W: www.abacusnetwork.co.uk

A cost efficient, quality service that meets all your needs is guaranteed, from year end & tax, through to being a part time Finance Director to help maximise your profits.

BJA Refrigeration Consulting Engineers Ltd

Derek Strokes 01484 680 069

Bridge Mills, Huddersfield Road,
Holmfirth, West Yorkshire HD9 3TW

F: 01484 680 041
E: derek@bjacool.co.uk
W: www.bjacool.co.uk

BJA are independent consultants offering professional and impartial advice to all users of refrigeration equipment and services including retailers, processors and manufacturers within the food and drink industry.

deliciously yorkshire

Specialist Services to the Food Industry

Colour It In

Mark Lancaster 01423 531 565

Unit 1 Hydro Business Park, Ripon Road,
Harrogate, North Yorkshire HG1 2BS

E: 01423 858 801
E: info@colouritin.co.uk
W: www.colouritin.co.uk

Colour It In is one of the regions most dynamic and forward thinking print companies. Based in Harrogate for over 15 years we specialise in helping companies to project the right image. Leaflets, brochures, signs, vehicle livery, POS, exhibition graphics - our friendly team are here to support your company.

CorpCom

Debbie Burman 01482 580 072

The Deep Business Centre, Hull,
East Yorkshire HU1 4BG

E: debby@corpcom.co.uk
W: www.corpcom.co.uk

CorpCom is a PR, marketing, events and design company based in Hull. With over 14 years' experience of working with food companies, large and small, we have found that the best way to sell your products is to get them to try it.

We specialise in organising masterclass and food demonstration events and have been successful in getting our clients into major retailers. We are also the organisers of the Hull Global Food Festival which will take place in August every year. Visit www.hullglobalfoodfest.co.uk

Design Futures

Andy Toward 01142 252 732

Sheffield Hallam University, Psalter Lane Campus,
Sheffield, South Yorkshire S11 8UZ

E: 01142 252 718
E: andy.toward@designfuturesgroup.com
W: www.designfuturesgroup.com

Design Futures is a centre of packaging expertise and innovative thinking - an ideas factory with practical output.

Accredited a Centre of Industrial Collaboration by Yorkshire Forward, it provides industry-focused research, design stratergy, brand positioning, innovative/ideas generation, structural packaging design, graphic design, technical authorship and training.

deliciouslyYorkshire

Specialist Services to the Food Industry

Edit Studios Limited

Ed Richardson 01423 541 812

29 Granville Road, Harrogate,
North Yorkshire HG1 1BY

E: ed@edit-studios.com
W: www.edit-studios.com

Business identity & website design, secure online shops, domain names, email & hosting, search engine optimisation.

Edit Studios is a specialist website design and development company providing a full range of internet services from small brochure websites through to fully automated secure online shopping facilities. Free initial consultation.

FDB Design Ltd

David Batty 0113 2300 111

COMMUNICATION...
THROUGH DESIGN
TAKING YOUR PRODUCT TO ITS HIGHEST POTENTIAL

Wharfegate, 24 River View, Boston Spa,
West Yorkshire LS23 6BA

F: 01132 300 112
E: david@fdbdesign.com
W: www.fdbdesign.com

Free consultancy to RFGYH members. FDB creates award winning design development and photography for packaging, label, logo, product branding, prototyping, design & mock-ups. Sales support: brochures, flyers, exhibition, marketing.

FDB was established in 1981 and creates top selling designs for a local and national client base, from a purpose built studio in Boston Spa overlooking the Wharfe.

For more information contact FDB direct and maximise your brand value!

Get Sorted Ltd

Andrew Lamb 08450 066 723

Get Sorted!

Get **Projects** Sorted!

Get **Innovation** Sorted!

Innovation Centre, Innovation Way,
Heslington, York, North Yorkshire YO10 5DG

E: andrew@getsortedmarketing.com
W: www.getsortedmarketing.com

A small but intimate marketing consultancy providing high quality marketing solutions for our clients. We enjoy rolling our sleeves up and delivering! We pride ourselves on commercial pragmatism linked to being ambitious for our clients. We enjoy the challenge and bringing our 25 years of food marketing experience to the party!

Specialist Services to the Food Industry

Gilholm Harrison Limited

Steve Gilholm   01904 795 869

Marlborough House, Westminster Place, York Business Park, Nether Poppleton, York, North Yorkshire YO26 6RW

F: 01904 795 382
E: steve.gilholm@gilholmharrison.com
W: www.gilholmharrison.com

Typically 80% of a company's value is its brand name. Gilholm Harrison is a firm of specialist attorneys who have experience in all aspects of intellectual property, including trade marks, registered designs and copyright.

We make applications for IP rights on behalf of clients and always explain costs and give a fixed price wherever possible. At least an hour's initial consultation is free of charge without obligation.

grasp - business development

Robin Norton   07941 129 025

50 Pannal Ash Grove, Harrogate, North Yorkshire HG2 0HZ

F: 01423 868 930
E: robin@grasp.org.uk
W: www.grasp.org.uk

Sell more food and drink, increase profits, develop your business. Get a better grasp of your customers, grasp more opportunities. Research, marketing and sales consultancy. Call for free practical advice.

Professionally

Harrison Goddard Foote

Cristina Rivas Graver   01132 330 100

Belgrave Hall, Belgrave Street, Leeds, West Yorkshire LS2 8DD

F: 01132 330 101
E: crgraver@hgf.com
W: www.hgf.com

HGF is one of the UK's leading firms of Patent and Trade Mark Attorneys with offices throughout the UK. We can help shape your IP strategy and assist in identifying how the IP affairs of your business are prioritised. We can also deal with the creation, identification and protection of IP and enhance its value to the business by appropriate management, exploitation and enforcement.
For further information, or for an initial consultation, please contact Jason Lumber on 01132 330 100 or email jlumber@hgf.com

Specialist Services to the Food Industry

Imagen Photography Ltd

Mark Kensett   01430 871 971

5 Becklands Park, York Road,
Market Weighton, East Yorkshire YO43 3GA

E: mark@imagenphotography.co.uk
W: www.imagenphotography.co.uk

Imagen are commercial photographers specialising in food for packaging, advertising, editorial, cookery books and PR.

We pride ourselves in our working relationship with our clients and on our creativity and expertise using the latest digital technology.

Our studios are both equiped with a full working kitchen, client lounge, ample parking and a warm friendly atmosphere.

Nelson Charles Management

Robert Bradley/Paul Rowntree   01132 824 226

Unit 223, 57 Great George Street,
Leeds, West Yorkshire LS1 3AJ

F: 08703 610 070
E: rob@nelsoncharles.com
W: www.nelsoncharles.com

Specialist consultants to the food and catering industry. If you are looking for experienced help in improving or establishing your business in any of the following fields then please contact us:

Menu and Product Development, Kitchen Design and Catering Equipment Procurement, Operations and Profit Maximization, Food Safety Consultancy and Training, Health and Safety Consultancy and Training, Event Catering and Management, Relief Chef Supply Service.

Lemon Zest

Jennifer Middleton   01757 268 283

Millbank, Water Row,
Cawood, North Yorkshire YO8 3SW

E: jennifer@lemonzestpr.co.uk
W: www.lemonzestpr.co.uk

Lemon Zest has built a reputation as one of the most effective small consultancies in the North of England.

Lemon Zest works hard to push the 'local is best' food message across Britain.

Powerhouse Photography

Neil Adams   01132 047 000

Rodley House Studio, Coal Hill Lane,
Rodley, West Yorkshire LS13 1DJ

F: 01132 047 000
E: neil@powerhousephoto.co.uk
W: www.powerhousephoto.co.uk

Powerhouse are specialists in food and drink photography. Our aim is to ensure that your product is represented in its most delicious and appetising way.

Specialist Services to the Food Industry

Red Squirrel Media

Suzanne Hudson   01943 468 282

Pegholme Mill, Wharfebank Business Centre,
Ilkley Road, Otley, West Yorkshire LS21 3JP

F: 01943 462 075
E: suzannehudson@redsquirrelmedia.co.uk
W: www.redsquirrelmedia.co.uk

An experienced and innovative design company committed to the environment and supporting local and worthwhile projects in our region.

5% of profits are donated to conservation.

Services include graphic design, web design, photography, multimedia and journalism.

Rollits Food Group

Julian Wild   01482 337 304

Wilberforce Court, High Street,
Hull, East Yorkshire HU1 1YJ

F: 08706 089 229
E: julian.wild@rollits.com
W: www.rollits.com

Rollits Food Group provides legal and commercial advice to food & drink companies, specialising in corporate, property and employment law.

Julian Wild has nearly 30 years experience of buying and selling food businesses, facilitating management buy-outs and financing transactions.

For more information call Julian on his mobile 07850 739 656.

Rubber Band Graphic Design

Peter Syson   01904 633 800

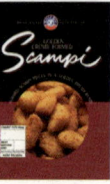

156a Haxby Road, York,
North Yorkshire YO31 8JP

F: 01904 633 201
E: peter@rubberbandisthe.biz
W: www.rubberbandisthe.biz

At Rubber Band we've done our stretch: over 25 years of successful, attractive marketing communications. Great graphics. Beautiful brochures. High impact ads. Prominent packaging. Wicked web work.

All for our clients. To make them and their brands look and sell better. Our experience and expertise are here for the taking: creative thinking supported by the latest technology. And an attitude that's recognised as going beyond the call of duty.

Specialist Services to the Food Industry

Sugar & Spice Food PRofiling and Marketing Specialists

Annie Stirk & Irene Myers   01347 810 531

Close House, Main Street, Stillington,
North Yorkshire YO61 1JU

E: anne.stirk@btopenworld.com / irene_myers@onetel.com
W: www.sugarandspicepr.co.uk

Serving up a recipe for success!

Irene and Annie are experienced and commited food media specialists, with a wealth of PR, marketing and consultancy 'know how'.

Through our passion for promoting and developing regional food, we have successfully raised the profile, and repositioned a whole host of Yorkshire food businesses.

Together, we can create a menu for your success...

Susan Kenyon Marketing Consultants Ltd

Sarah Banton   01484 437 424

Unit 59A, The Media Centre, Huddersfield,
West Yorkshire HD1 4QX

F: 01484 437 426
E: info@susankenyon.co.uk
W: www.susankenyon.co.uk

ASK Strategic Marketing & Research specialists in Food & Drink, Health & Well-Being products.

Market Research, Marketing Plans, Marketing 'Clinics', New Brand/Product Development and Public Relations.

2007 Consumer insight projects include: Fruit/Veg/Salad Eating habits/Organic Produce/VMS & Functional Foods.

Sycamore

Paul Wells   01904 567 670

The IT Centre, York Science Park,
York, North Yorkshire YO10 5DG

F: 01904 567 672
E: paul@sycamore-uk.com
W: www.sycamore-uk.com

Design, Websites, Marketing, PR, Signage.

Tanfield Engineering

Kari Bosworth/Bill Bates   01677 423 370

Tutin Road, Leeming Bar Industrial Estate,
Northallerton, North Yorkshire DL7 9UJ

F: 01677 423 370
E: tanfieldengineer@btconnect.com
W: www.tanfieldengineering.co.uk

We offer specialist engineering services to the food, brewing and dairy industries, including the manufacture, maintenance, repair or reconditioning of all process equipment. Individual maintenance contracts available.

Specialist Services to the Food Industry

The Lock 23

Nick Lock 01132 425 234

Suite A4 Joseph's Well, Hanover Walk,
Leeds, West Yorkshire LS3 1AB

E: nick@thelock23.co.uk
W: www.thelock23.co.uk

'Unlocking more sales'

The Lock 23 are brand packaging design specialists. Packaging is the key point at which your brand touches your customer and we have over 20 years experience of influencing purchasing decisions.

If you want to get more customers to pick your brand from the shelf then you need to talk to us.

Thru the Line

Erika Ritchie 01132 577 999

21 Holly Park Mills, Woodhall Road, Calverley,
Leeds, West Yorkshire LS28 5QS

F: 01132 570 695
E: erika.ritchie@thrutheline.com
W: www.thrutheline.com

As winner of the Design Business Effectiveness Awards 2007, we believe that any of our communication has to be creative, effective and measurable. Supporting our clients every step of the way, whether your brief is to:- Create a new brand identity; Design new packaging or sales promotional collateral and mock ups; Research your market place; Raise awareness of your product; increase footfall; Develop meaningful relationships with buyers.

99.9% of our business is referred to us.

TM Project Solutions Ltd

Norman O'Riley 01757 282 250

Manor Farm, Main Street,
Bubwith, East Yorkshire YO8 6LT

F: 01757 282 251
E: sales@tmpsolutions.co.uk
W: www.tmpsolutions.co.uk

TMPS deliver solutions tailor-made to meet your process and production needs.

Our experienced team provides a range of flexible engineering sevices designed to support the core resources of its clients.

From concept through design to implementation. We can deliver your project to budget, to specification and on time.

Calendar of Foodie Events

January
Farmhouse Breakfast Week

February
Wakefield International Festival of Rhubarb

April
York Easter Market
Harrogate Spring Flower Show

May
Ryedale Festival of Food and Drink
Dales Festival of Food and Drink, Leyburn

June
Lincolnshire Show
Broughton Hall Game Fair

July
Great Yorkshire Show
Driffield Show
Ryedale Show
CLA Game Fair (every three years)

August
Yorkshire Day
Emley Show
Bingley Show
Egton Show

September
Harrogate Flower Festival
York Festival of Food and Drink

October
Countryside Live

November
Deliciouslyorkshire Annual Awards
Crafts for Christmas
St Nicholas' Fair

December
Knaresborough Christmas Market

For the latest show information, please visit www.deliciouslyorkshire.co.uk

The Regional Food Group

rfg|YH
The Regional Food Group for Yorkshire and Humber

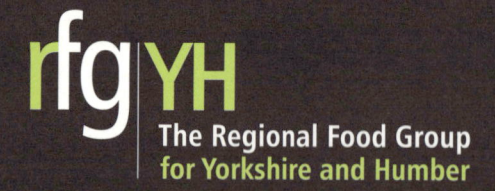

About The Regional Food Group and our Funders

The Regional Food Group for Yorkshire and Humber is dedicated to acting on behalf of all those companies committed to fantastic food and drink from Yorkshire and Humber.

Funded and supported by Yorkshire Forward and Food from Britain, the RFGYH is a non-for profit company and custodian of the Deliciouslyorkshire campaigning brand.

Established to promote and raise awareness of food and drink produced within Yorkshire and Humber, the organisation has worked with more than 700 businesses in the region since it was founded in July 2005.

The group provides a one stop shop for all trade, consumer and media enquiries as well as a support network for the industry. The group comprises three unified specialist divisions designed to service the complete needs of the region's food and drink industry members. The divisions include Commercial, Technology (formerly FTAS) and Skills (formerly TeamFood).

Supported by Yorkshire Forward, The Region's Development Agency

Food from Britain

This project is part-financed by the European Regional Development Fund

Want to know more?

Big Barn Promotes local, seasonal food and supports British Farmers, Tel 01234 871005. www.bigbarn.co.uk

FARMA – National Farmers' Retail and Markets Association – a co-operative of UK farmers, producers and farmers markets. Tel 0245 458 8420. www.farma.org.uk

Farm Retail Association (formerly the Farm Shop and Pick your Own Association). Lists farm shops and PYOs throughout the UK. Tel 02380 362150. Visit www.farmshopping.com

Food From Britain A guide to more than 3,000 regional food and drink producers in the UK Tel 020 7233 5111. www.foodfrombritain.com/regional

Regional Food Group for Yorkshire and Humber Not-for-profit membership organisation promoting food and drink from the region via its Deliciouslyorkshire brand.

For comprehensive (and frequently updated) list of producers, hotels, bed & breakfast, caterers, delis and independent retailers and farm shops. Tel 01937 830354. www.deliciouslyorkshire.co.uk or www.rfgyh.co.uk

The National Association of Farmers Markets Established to help local producers sell goods direct to the public locally. Tel 01225 787914. See www.farmersmarkets.net for details of your nearest market.

Country Markets Weekly markets are run as a non-profit making co-operative. Tel 01246 261508. Check www.country-markets.co.uk for your nearest market.

Yorkshire Tourist Board Information on places to visit and stay. Tel 01904 707961. www.yorkshire.com

Alphabetical Index

A

17 Burgate	168
42 The Calls	180
A L Simpkin & Co Ltd	108
a really cool company	187
Aarhus Karlshamn	129
Abacus 155 Ltd	187
Ackroyds Restaurants Meats	97
Ainsty Farm Shop	95
Amos Kaye	109
Ampleforth Abbey	72
Andrew Jones Pies	153
Andrew M Jackson	187
Angel Chocolates	64
Apricot Lodge	168
Areolives	155
Arthur Haigh Ltd	59,79
Ascot Lodge Guest House	168
Ashberry Hotel	168
Ashmount Guest House	180
At Home	91

B

Bagel Nash	148
Bank Villa	56,169
Bare Earth	84
Barker Stakes Farm	169
Baytree House	169
Beacon Farm Ice Cream	67
Beadlam Grange Farmshop & Tearoom	95
Beef Improvement Grouping Ltd	130
Bettys & Taylors of Harrogate	87,344
BJA Refrigeration Consulting Engineers Ltd	187
Black Sheep Brewery	56,72
Blacker Hall Farm Shop	160
Bleiker's Smokehouse Ltd	50,375
Blue Keld Springs Ltd	123,128
Bootham Gardens Guesthouse	169
Boutique Catering	159
Bow House Limited	187
Brazilian Flavours	141,155
Brooklands Guest House	169
Broom House	170
Brown Eggs Ltd	68
Burton Agnes Hall Farmers Food Store	123,135

C

Café Harlequin	88
Carricks Fish Ltd	91
Castle Howard Farm Shop	95
Catherine's Choice	113
Cedar Court - Harrogate	170
Cedar Court - Bradford	181
Cedar Court - Huddersfield	181
Cedar Court - Wakefield	181
Charlottes Jersey Ice Cream Ltd	149
Chaucer Foods Ltd	132
Cheese & Co	64
Chippindale Foods Ltd	68
Choc-Affair	64
Clocktower at Rudding Park	40,170
Colin M Robinson	79
Colour It In	188
Cooplands	104,108
Coppice House Farm Shop Rivelin	116
Cornscape	111
CorpCom	188
Costello's Ltd	134
Country Fresh Foods	117
Country Products Limited	78
Cropton Brewery	43,72
Crown Hotel	105,114
Cryer & Stott	48,160
Cucina	160
Cundall Lodge Farm B&B	170
Cunninghams Foods Ltd	103,114
Curry Cuisine	157

D

D. Westwood & Son	151
D.C.H & The Court Café-Bistro & Bar	88
Davill's Patisserie	57,64
Dean Court Hotel	171
Debbie & Andrew's	16,61,79
De'Clare	91
Delicious Alchemy	108
Denholme Gate Apiary	142,157
Design Futures	188
Dimple Well Lodge	181
Dolce Vita	65
Dore Delicatessen	103,116
Dunsley Hall Country House Hotel	171

E

E.Oldroyd & Sons Ltd	11,49,151
East Riding Country Pork	130
Edit Studios Limited	189
Elizabeth Botham & Sons	65
Elizabeth Smedley Speciality Foods	57,86
Elmfield House	172
English Village Salads Ltd	76

F

Far Isle Farm (Formerly S&C Meats)	152
Farmer Copleys	161
Farmhouse Preserves	86
Farrah's Harrogate Toffee	65
FDB Design Ltd	189
Field House B&B	181
Food Design	78
Food for Thought Ltd	115
Fosters Bakery Ltd	108
Fountains Abbey & Studley Royal	88
Four Gables	181
Foxton Country Fresh	129
Fruitface Fresh Nutrition	132
Funky Snack Company	132
Future Fresh Ltd	76

G

Gallon House	171
George and Dragon	172
Get Sorted Ltd	189
Gilholm Harrison Limited	190
Glenroyd House Preserves	113
Gordon Rhodes & Son	152
Grandma Wilds Biscuits	148
Granny's Kitchen	158
grasp - business development	190
Grassington Lodge	172
Greens	88
Grimston House	172
GW Price	111

H

Hambleton Ales	45,56,73
Harrison Goddard Foote	190
Hellaby Hall Hotel	114
Henshelwoods Delicatessen	91
Herbs Unlimited	61,76
Hider Foods Imports Ltd	136
High Catton Grange - B&B & Self Catering	180
Holdsworth House	182
Holme Farmed Venison	80
Holme House	182
Hornby Castle	80
Hotel Du Vin	172
Humdinger Ltd	129

Alphabetical Index

I
Ideal Lincs Ltd 165
Ilkley Moor Vaults 145,159
Imagen Photography Ltd 191
Independent Foods (I's Pies) 57,83
Inglenook Guest House 173
Inspired Eating 115
It's Nut Free 65

J
J A Carlile Farms Ltd 127
J E Hartley 77
J H & M Burton 131
J. Lord & Son
'Take & Bake' Ltd 142,153
Johnson's Toffees 148
Just Puds Limited 121,126

K
Keelham Hall Farm Shop 143,161
Kelleythorpe Farm Shop 135
King Asia Foods Ltd 112
Kings Square Café 173
Kitchen 126
Kitchen Guru 133

L
L H Fine Foods 92
Lamb-In-A-Box 131
Langlands Farm Shop 136
Langthorne's Buffalo Produce 80
Lemon Tree 150
Lemon Zest 191
Lewis & Cooper Ltd 17,92
Lishmans of Ilkley
(York Ham & Sausage Co.) 144,153
Little Weghill Farm 180
Lockwoods 173
Love Bites Foods 143,155

Lovesome Hill Farm 173
Low Leases Organic Farm 77
Low Penhowe 13,173
Lowna Dairy Ltd 127

M
M A Worsdale 73
Mackenzies Yorkshire
Smokehouse 14,81
Malmaison 182
Manor Farm Shop 136
Manor Guest House 183
McCallums Bank End
Farm Shop 104,117
Metcalfe Organic 77
Mill Close Farm 174
Morley's of Swanland 135
Mount Pleasant Hotel 105,115
Mr Moo's Real Dairy
Ice Cream 123,128

N
Nelson Charles Management 191
New Inn Hotel 174
Newton House 174
Northern Select Foods Ltd 47,98

O
Organic Dales 149

P
Park Lodge Farm 77
Pattacakes 126
Payne's Dairy Ltd 68
Peacocks Desserts 60,66
Peasholm Park Hotel 174
Phoenix Court 174
Pickersgill Manor Farm B&B 183
Pie & Ltd 154
Pipers Crisps 165

Pollards Tea & Coffee 103, 110
Potts Bakers Ltd 109
Powerhouse Photography 191
Proudfoot Group 93
Punjabi Curry Sauce
Company 105, 112

Q
Quality Greens 98

R
Radisson SAS 183
Rafi's Spicebox 92
Rags Hotel Bar and Restaurant ... 180
Rawcliffe House Farm 175
Raydale Preserves 86
Rebori 133
Red Chard Grill Rooms 89
Red Lea Hotel 175
Red Squirrel Media 192
Redcliffe Farm Shop and Café 96
Redhill Farm Free Range Pork 165
Ridings of Yorkshire 149
Ripley Ice Cream 93
Ripley Store 93
Robinsons Pork Butchers
Knaresborough Ltd 81
Rollits Food Group 192
Rombalds Hotel & Restaurant 183
Rose Cottage Foods Ltd 123,131
Rosebud Cottage Guest House ... 184
Rosebud Preserves 57,87
Round Green Farm
Venison Company 103,110
Rubber Band Graphic Design 192
Ryeburn of Helmsley 69

S
Santeau 73
Seabrook Crisps Ltd 143,156

Seamer Fayre 81
Shaws of Huddersfield Ltd 158
Sheff's Special 114
Shepcote Distributors 122,130
Shepherds Purse Cheeses Ltd .. 60,69
Side Oven Bakery 122,126
Simply Chocolate 66
Simpson's 129
Sloe Motion 73
Smugglers Rock Country House .. 175
Soup Dragons (Bon Bouche) 156
Spindleberry Inns 89
Splash Winery Ltd 150
Stamfrey Farm Organics 15,69
Stoney End Holidays 175
Strawberry House 175
Stuart's Foods Ltd 78
Sugar & Spice Food PRofiling
and Marketing Specialists 193
Sunnybank 184
Susan Kenyon Marketing
Consutants Ltd 193
Sutcliffe Farmers Ltd 111
Swaledale Cheese Company 46,70
Swales Yorkshire Dales
Ice Cream 70
Sweets on the Menu 109
Swinton Park 56,175
Sycamore 193

T
Tanfield Engineering 193
Tarts and Titbits 93
Taste Tradition Ltd 60,82
The Almar 176
The Austwick Traddock 89
The Bakery 66
The Balloon Tree Farm
Shop & Café 96

Alphabetical Index

The Boars Head Hotel &
Ripley Castle 176
The Carlton Lodge 176
The Chocolate Factory Ltd 66
The Crown Hotel 105,114
The Crusty Pie Company 154
The Denby Dale Pie Co. 154
The Devonshire Arms
Country House Hotel and Spa 176
The Devonshire Fell Hotel &
Restaurant 176
The Dusty Miller 184
The Essential Food &
Drink Company Limited 110
The Farmer's Cart 18,96
The Forge Farm Shop &
Sandwich Bar 97
The Gallery 59,176
The General Tarleton 38,90
The Ginger Pig Shop 94
The Golden Fleece 59,177
The Grand St Ledger Hotel 179
The Grange Hotel 177
The Harmony Guest House 177
The Helen Francis Cake
Company 149
The Huddersfield Central Lodge .. 185
The Inn at Hawnby 90
The Keld Head Springs Ltd 74
The Kimberley Hotel 177
The Kings Head Hotel
and Restaurant 177
The Little Chocolate Shop Ltd 67
The Lock 23 194
The Lodge at Leeming Bar 178
The Old Registry 184
The Old Town Hall Guest
House & Tea Room 178
The Organic Pantry 97

The Pipe and Glass Inn 12,121,134
The Plough Inn At Wigglesworth .. 178
The Poplars 179
The Punch Brew Co 74
The Railway Hotel 185
The Real Bradford Curry
Company 143,156
The Real Bread Bakehouse Ltd 109
The Real Yorkshire Pudding
Company Ltd 112
The Salad Garden (York) Ltd 84
The Star Inn 37,90
The Star Inn Speciality Foods 85
The Topping Pie Company 105,111
The Ultimate Candy
Company Limited 127
The Wensleydale Creamery 70
The White Swan Inn 178
The Yorkshire Provender 57,85
Thorncroft Ltd 74
Thorpe Park Hotel & Spa 159
Thru the Line 194
Tickton Grange 121,134
TM Project Solutions Ltd 194
Tower House Executive
Guest House 185
True Foods 57,85

U
Ulrick & Short 44, 152

V
Vale of Mowbray Ltd 83
Voakes Pies 19,84

W
W S Bentley (Growers) Ltd 151
Watermill House B&B 179
Watermill Restaurant
(Milford Hotel) 185

Weeton's 94
Well House 179
Wentworth Brewery Ltd 110
Wharfe Valley Cheesecakes
Limited 67
Wharfe Valley Farms 158
White Rose Preserves 87
Whole Hog Sausage Company 82
Wilkinson Butchers Ltd 105,116
William Jackson & Son Ltd 132
Wilsons of Crossgates 154
Wold Top Brewery 122,128
Womersley Fine Foods Ltd 158
Woodhead Bakers Ltd 67
Wynnstay House 179

Y
Yoghurt Delights 71
Yorkshire Cider 75
Yorkshire Country Wines 75
Yorkshire Crisp Company 103,113
Yorkshire Dales Cheese
Company 94
Yorkshire Dales Meat
Company 42,82
Yorkshire Farmhouse Eggs 61,71
Yorkshire Game Ltd 83
Yorkshire Hemp Limited 133
Yorkshire Hills 150
Yorvale 71
Yummy Yorkshire Ice Cream
Company (P. Holmes & Son) 150

Z
Zeina Foods 157